THE STORY OF BEGINNINGS

The Story of Beginnings

Listening to the Bible's Introduction

H. MARK ABBOTT

WIPF & STOCK · Eugene, Oregon

THE STORY OF BEGINNINGS
Listening to the Bible's Introduction

Copyright © 2013 H. Mark Abbott. All rights reserved. Except for brief quotations in critical publications or reviews, no part of this book may be reproduced in any manner without prior written permission from the publisher. Write: Permissions, Wipf and Stock Publishers, 199 W. 8th Ave., Suite 3, Eugene, OR 97401
Primary Scripture translation used is NRSV.

Wipf & Stock
An Imprint of Wipf and Stock Publishers
199 W. 8th Ave., Suite 3
Eugene, OR 97401

www.wipfandstock.com

ISBN: 978-1-61097-015-0

Manufactured in the U.S.A.

Contents

Acknowledgments | vii

1. What's So Important About Introductions? | 1
2. A Story | 13
3. God | 28
4. God Created | 44
5. God Created Image Bearers | 57
6. God Created Humans for Love | 74
7. The Blessing of Sabbath | 88
8. The Tempter | 100
9. Rebellion Against Love | 113
10. Good News of Hope | 127

Bibliography | 137

Acknowledgments

MY HEARTFELT THANKS TO the two western New York churches, and to the Seattle, Washington, congregation, where all together I served for forty-two years as a preaching pastor! With these church folk, I turned again and again to the opening chapters of the Bible for light on what God's creative intent was and is for the creation—especially for the human creation.

I'm especially grateful for the privilege of serving First Free Methodist Church in Seattle for twenty-eight years. As the campus church of Seattle Pacific University, FFMC gave me access to a faith-based, academic community in which important questions are encouraged rather than squelched. I'm grateful for the opportunity I had to explore weighty issues, such as those raised in Genesis 1–3, and to discuss them openly and graciously. It marked a pleasant contrast to the occasionally acrimonious interaction such issues can bring.

I'm not a scientist, historian, or academic theologian, and I don't write primarily for the academic community. However, I'm thankful for the scientists, historians, and theologians whose writings helped me to understand how devout believers can be, at the same time, both fully open to science and true to Scripture. I've tried to use these authors

Acknowledgments

to help me pastorally bridge the gap that often exists between the academic and church communities. I'm relieved and delighted that these days there's an increased willingness on the part of devoted believers to approach the issues of creation with greater openness and with less fear, which used to keep many in bondage.

Thanks also to Reece Carson for straightening out my prose and fixing my punctuation. While keeping my own voice intact, he brought these chapters into line and made my use of language more consistent. I'm grateful!

My thanks to Mary Ann, my wife of forty-seven years, who encourages me to invest some of my time during these retirement years into putting some of what I have preached into writing.

1

What's So Important About Introductions?

ONE PUBLISHER CLAIMS THAT by the time he's finished reading the first paragraph he knows whether a manuscript is worth publishing. Opening paragraphs, whether fiction or nonfiction, should hook readers into staying with the author as the plot or theme unfolds. I sometimes tell students of the art of preaching that we have two minutes maximum to hook listeners' attention in Sunday sermons. I've been known to overstate that case by quoting one Hollywood recipe for a good movie: "Start with an earthquake and build to a climax!"

MEMORABLE FIRST LINES.

Remember the way Charles Dickens began *A Tale of Two Cities*? "It was the best of times, it was the worst of times..." Another memorable first line from Dickens, this time from *A Christmas Carol*: "Marley was dead: to begin with."

The Bible isn't fiction. The introduction to the Bible isn't just a "hook." But few introductions anywhere are more promising, more powerful, and more pregnant with mystery and meaning. Eugene Peterson's *The Message* renders ancient language in direct, contemporary ways that reach out and grab us. Listen to its opening sentences of Genesis:

> First this: God created the Heavens and Earth—all you see, all you don't see. Earth was a soup of nothingness, a bottomless emptiness, an inky blackness. God's Spirit brooded like a bird above the watery abyss.

My reaction is, "Wow! I want more!"

The introduction to the Bible isn't only powerful language; it's also basic for everything that follows in the book. In fact, the Bible's introduction is basic for life.

Some scholars extend the Bible's introduction through the Noah story; that is, to Genesis 11. But Genesis 1–3 introduces the core themes and key characters of the Bible. Here we meet God, humans, and the tempter. Here we encounter human rebellion against the Lover-God, the consequences of such rebellion, and a glimmer of hope regarding what God will do about it. Therefore, it's the first three chapters of the Bible that I'm treating as its introduction.

THEMATIC SEEDS IN ITS OPENING PAGES ECHO THROUGHOUT THE ENTIRE BIBLE.

As Eugene Peterson puts it in his introduction to Genesis in *The Message*, "Genesis gets us off on the right foot. Genesis pulls us into a sense of reality that is God-shaped and God-filled."[1]

As we read through the Bible, we'll be referred back periodically, whether explicitly or implicitly, to its opening chapters. Genesis starts this way: "In the beginning, God

1. Peterson, "Introduction to Genesis."

created . . ." Doesn't that remind us of another creation-linked beginning, this time in the Gospel of John? "In the beginning was the Word, and the Word was with God, and the Word was God" (John 1:1). As we shall see in a few moments, Jesus and the Apostle Paul also refer their hearers and readers back to the Bible's introduction.

Furthermore, the introduction to the Bible links us with this great book's conclusion. Genesis and Revelation are powerful bookends to the Bible's great story. Creation looks forward to the not-yet-experienced New Creation. The garden of Genesis 1–3 anticipates the garden in the city that's described in the final two chapters of the Bible. "Then I saw a new heaven and a new earth; for the first heaven and the first earth had passed. . . . And I saw the holy city, the New Jerusalem, coming down out of heaven from God" (Rev. 21:1–2).

Skim over the Bible's introduction and you'll risk missing the impact of the whole Bible!

TWO BASIC LENSES FOR UNDERSTANDING THE BIBLE: COVENANT AND CREATION.

Certainly the whole Bible is important. As Scripture, the Bible is "inspired by God and useful . . ." (2 Tim. 3:16). But an important lens through which we read the Bible is the person, words, and work of Jesus. All sections of the Bible point to Jesus. Jesus is at the core of *covenant*—new covenant. We understand the whole Bible through the lens of Jesus.

Interacting with hostile religious leaders, Jesus said, "You search the scriptures because you think that in them you have eternal life; and it is they that testify of me. . . . If you believed Moses, you would believe me, for he wrote about me" (John 5:39, 46). In the gripping post-resurrection story set on the road to Emmaus, Luke tells how Jesus "beginning with Moses and all the prophets, interpreted

The Story of Beginnings

to them the things about himself in all the scriptures" (Luke 24:27). It's on Jesus' authority that we read the Bible through the lens of Jesus.

However, the other key lens, also basic to the way we read and understand the Bible, is in Genesis 1–3. In this introduction to the Bible, we go behind the theme of covenant to that of *creation*. Here, we're introduced to a progression: from creation to fall to redemption (or re-creation). To put it in nontheological language, Genesis 1–3 is about what God intended for the cosmos and for humans, about how humans messed up, and about what God is going to do about it.

One theology professor's slogan I heard was, "Where you begin in theology determines where you end up." While we understand the Bible through the lens of Jesus, the book doesn't begin with Jesus. The book begins with God's acts of creation. But the work of Christ is hinted at in what is sometimes called the *protoevangelium*, the first gospel, in Genesis 3:15. Here is the picture of ongoing enmity between the human and the adversary, pictured in chapter 3 as a serpent. The storyteller, however, hints at what is to come in the rest of the Bible's great story. "He [a descendant of Adam] will strike your [the serpent's] head, and you will strike his heel."

The great story of the Bible reaches its climax at the end of the book of Revelation and the final defeat of the adversary (Rev. 20). Then there comes New Creation! "The one who was seated on the throne said, 'See, I am making all things new'" (Rev. 21:5). Where we begin determines where we end up. Creation, fall, re-creation are the great themes of the Bible, embedded in its introduction.

What's So Important About Introductions?

I KEEP RETURNING, AGAIN AND AGAIN, TO THE THEMES OF GENESIS 1–3.

I'm not an academic theologian, or a professional historian, or a scientist. But I was a pastor for forty-two years—twenty-eight years in one congregation—and an adjunct seminary teacher of homiletics for many of those years. I write not primarily for academicians, but for ordinary churchgoers, for people who want to know who they are and what God wants them to do. Genesis 1–3 has shaped my life, my thinking, and my preaching. I've come to the conviction that these opening chapters of the Bible establish key themes in a believer's basic worldview. The following basic Bible themes will be opened up in the chapters of this book:

- What kind of literature is the Bible's introduction, and how shall we read it?
- What is God, the creator, like?
- How shall we understand the Creator-God's work and respond to it?
- What's so unique about the human creation? And for what purposes were humans created?
- What did God intend by blessing Sabbath?
- What happened between the tempter, depicted as a serpent, and Adam and Eve?
- How did Adam and Eve offend their Creator-Friend, and how does that impact us today?
- How does God give us a hint of what God is doing about that?

In each chapter, I'll suggest a contemporary life application for those who would take seriously this introduction to the Bible. For example, in the chapter "God," I point to worship

The Story of Beginnings

as the appropriate response to the revelation of who the Creator-God is.

I'M IN GOOD COMPANY WHEN I RETURN OFTEN TO GENESIS 1–3.

What did Jesus do when religious leaders asked him a trick question about whether or not divorce was acceptable? Jesus referred his questioners back to the Bible's introduction. "Have you not read . . . ?" said Jesus to the Pharisees. Imagine Jesus posing that question to Jewish religious leaders! That's like asking contemporary pastors if they ever read the Bible! "Have you not read that the one who made them at the beginning 'made them male and female?'" Jesus then quoted further from Genesis 1:27: "For this reason a man shall leave his father and mother and be joined to his wife, and the two shall become one flesh" (Matt. 19:4–5). Jesus pointed to the Bible's introduction as key to understanding this and other important issues in life.

In his insightful treatment of how to read and understand the Bible today, scholar and churchman N. T. Wright makes this comment on Jesus' use of Genesis 1: "Jesus is saying that we are to read scriptures as the story of creation and new creation, and to read the specific codes of the Old Testament as provisional and temporary means to that larger end." Wright continues to observe that Genesis and the New Testament's use of it make the case that "the original creation was good and the creator God is in the business of remaking it." In fact, says Wright, referring to the entire Bible, "the renewal of creation through Jesus Christ is the key theme of the whole story."[2] There's more in the final chapter of this book on this renewal-of-creation theme embedded in the Bible's introduction.

2. Wright, *Scripture and Authority*, 188–90.

What's So Important About Introductions?

The Apostle Paul returns to the same passage in the Bible's introduction that Jesus did. Writing to the Ephesian church about the Christian household, Paul cites Genesis 2 and its reference to a man leaving father and mother and cleaving to his wife: "And the two shall become one flesh." Then, Paul adds, "This is a great mystery, and I am applying it to Christ and the church" (Eph. 5:31–32).

The early church fathers, those closest to Jesus and the apostles, honored and used the opening chapters of the Bible. In *Ancient Christian Commentary on Scripture*, Andrew Louth, editor of this multivolume series, highlights how the church fathers invested major significance in the early chapters of Genesis. In fact, Louth writes, "The Fathers read the first chapters of the Bible as unfolding a theological understanding of the human condition."[3]

Louth identifies central themes in the early church fathers, which they found highlighted in Genesis 1–3. These key theological themes include:

- *Adam and Christ.* "If the significance of Christ is summed up through . . . contrast between him and Adam, then the account of Adam himself assumed archetypal significance for understanding the fallen human condition."

- *Typology.* "The tragic parallelism of Adam and Christ became a key to understanding Christ's significance: Adam's disobedience is matched by Christ's obedience, the tree of the knowledge of good and evil is matched by the tree/wood of the cross . . . Eve is matched by Mary . . ."

- *Creation.* Louth cites key fourth-century church leader Athanasius: "As we proceed in our exposition of this [the incarnation of the Word], we must first speak

3. Louth, *Ancient Christian Commentary*, lii.

about the creation of the universe and its creator, God, so that in this way we may consider as fitting that its renewal was effected by the Word who created it in the beginning."

- *Humanity in the image of God.* These early leaders linked the *imago dei*—the image of God in the human creation—with God's purpose to transform believers into the image of Christ. "Human beings are created in the image of God and, finally transfigured by the glory of God, will display God's likeness."[4]

The introduction to the Bible in Genesis 1–3 was important to Jesus, to Paul, and to early post-apostolic church leaders. It certainly must be important to us.

WHAT ARE MY GOALS IN WRITING THIS BOOK?

I want to highlight the importance of a creation-based vision for today's Christ-followers. Much of Christian theology and practical Christian living revolves around the theme of covenant. Covenant *is* crucial. But we neglect the theme of creation to our detriment and to the detriment of the creation, which came from God's hands and is entrusted to the stewardship of God's human creation. As with any good introduction, this basic theme is embedded in the book's opening pages.

While I recognize and use the prolific scholarly resources on Genesis, this isn't a book designed primarily for academicians. My purpose is to accept the Bible's introduction on its own terms. That will mean learning to listen for what it said to its first hearers and readers, not just imposing

---

4. Ibid., xlvii.

What's So Important About Introductions?

our modern and very different points of view on the ancient text. This will require that I offer insights from scholars to help us understand how to listen to this ancient story.

For example, I recognize the scholarly work regarding the authorship and dating of Genesis. I accept the perspective that Genesis is a composite document, rather than a single volume written by Moses as was traditionally understood. This composite document's final form, says Walter Brueggemann, "is a product of and response to the Babylonian exile." This representative Old Testament scholar, among many others, recognizes that materials older than Israel's exile were used in this composite document. But "the exilic or postexilic location of the final form of the text suggests that the Old Testament materials . . . are to be taken precisely in an acute crisis of displacement, when old certitudes . . . had failed."[5] If we accept this view, it frames how we—who also live in an era in which "old certitudes" have failed—hear this ancient text. We hear and respond not only to the question of origins ("Where did things come from?"), but also of identity ("Who are we anyway?").

Readers may come to different conclusions on the validity of scholarly positions about authorship and dating. But, we still should listen carefully to this remarkable story, and listen as closely as possible to what the ancient text is saying.

Furthermore, I want to diffuse frequent contemporary tensions in creation issues by refocusing our primary attention on these opening segments of the Bible as story, true story, rather than as science and history. We'll not ignore questions about evolution or about whether or not Adam and Eve were literal human beings. My intention is to summarize and make some of the more recent scholarship relating to these themes more accessible to the average Bible reader. My purpose, however, isn't to prove or disprove

5. Brueggemann, *Theology of Old Testament*, 74–75.

commonly held views regarding the *how* and the *when* of creation. Rather, we'll move beyond those contemporary and often contentious issues to what this ancient story is most basically telling us.

As a pastor among well-educated people, I've found myself periodically in the middle of controversy regarding creation issues. At times, I've interacted with folks who had come to believe that their faith and trust in the Bible depended on disproving evolution. I've encouraged such people to be cautious about drawing a line in the sand too firmly here, and about making the Bible say what it may not be saying. With others, the tendency has been to debunk the creation account, emptying it of meaning for today. With them, I've reiterated the Bible's truth, but truth not as we understand it from history and science.

I also want to help us live as God's image bearers. While we're damaged by our relational separation from the Creator-God, all humans are still image bearers. There may be no single factor more important in shaping our interaction with other men and women, believers and nonbelievers, saints and sinners, people we like and people we don't like, than whether or not we have a deep awareness of the imago dei. If Genesis, in fact, comes out of the period of Israel's exile in Babylon, one of its primary messages for today is about who people of faith are and what they should be doing while living in a culture that doesn't share that faith. These were key exilic issues then as they are today, some twenty-five hundred years later.

Finally, I want to point toward the hope hinted at in the introduction to the Bible. This is hope fulfilled in the second Adam, Jesus, whose purpose is to re-create human beings and re-create the cosmos. This vision of what God through the Son and the Spirit is about today motivates our lives of faith, love, and service.

What's So Important About Introductions?

One of my favorite hymns is "Love Divine, All Loves Excelling," by Charles Wesley. In it, Wesley reaches this hope-filled, New-Creation climax:

> Finish, then, thy new creation, pure and spotless let us be.
> Let us see thy great salvation perfectly restored in thee;
> Changed from glory into glory, till in heaven we take our place,
> Till we cast our crowns before thee, lost in wonder, love, and praise.

WHAT, THEN, IS SO IMPORTANT ABOUT INTRODUCTIONS—ESPECIALLY THIS INTRODUCTION TO THE BIBLE?

The Bible's introduction shines light on what is of ultimate importance in the entire book: namely, the Creator-God and the Creator-God's love affair with creation. It makes crystal clear how human beings are to look at ourselves and at other members of God's human creation. It introduces the basic story lines, which, like musical themes, are played out as God's great story unfolds. It sets the stage for all that follows, portraying in story form the foundational realities that shape life even today.

On a Sunday during Advent, while writing this book, I saw two actors portray the story of Jesus' birth using words of Scripture almost exclusively. They began, however, not just with words from the gospels, but also with Genesis 1–3. It reminded me that we understand Jesus' birth in the context of what the Creator-God did "in the beginning." We understand the whole Bible in the context of its introduction.

The Story of Beginnings

However, to get a handle on what this introduction to the Bible tells us, we have to understand what Genesis 1–3 is and what it is not. What kind of literary genre is it? What impact does that question have on how we should read and understand these basic and introductory paragraphs of our Bible? And how do we avoid misusing this ancient text by imposing our twenty-first-century ideas on it? These are the themes of the next chapter, "A Story."

2

A Story

Several years ago, I was teaching on the importance of Genesis 1–3 with a large group of pastors in the central African nation Burundi. Frequently, I used the word *story* to describe what we find in the Bible's introduction. Not long into the teaching, the African bishop, who was well versed in English and seated in the front row, spoke up. "When you say the word 'story' the translator is using the Kirundi word for 'myth.' Is that what you mean?" asked the bishop. I saw in their context that myth meant a story that isn't true. I assured him that when I was talking about the Genesis story, I understood it to be a *true* story. We continued with the translator using the word for *record*. While that wasn't quite what I had in mind, it seemed better than what they understood by myth.

Though the Greek word *mythos* doesn't typically mean false, this is the way we often use that word. By contrast, as Seattle Pacific University Professor Eugene Lemcio points out, myth "originally referred to an explanatory story, where the divine world was involved with the world of human affairs."[1]

STORY IS A POWERFUL CONVEYER OF TRUTH.

In an online column, Steve Denning, who's been called "the Warren Buffet of business communication," suggests this definition of story: "To say what something means is to say how it is related or connected to something else. To ask the meaning of an event is to ask how it contributed to the story in which it occurs. It is the connections or relations between events."[2] In other words, story communicates meaning.

To call something a story doesn't mean it's unreliable, as in "he's just telling you a story," or "that's a lie," or "that can't be trusted!" Often, when we want to make a case for the truth of something, we'll say, "Let me tell you a story." In fact, some of the greatest communicators in history—from Homer to Abraham Lincoln to C. S. Lewis—have been storytellers. And even today, many modernists and postmodernists are recapturing the wonder of story as a vehicle for truth.

The whole Bible is one grand story made up of multiple shorter stories. And this grand story of the Bible, as well as the introduction to the whole book, is true. However, a modern way of thinking often attributes truth only to what we call data. That is, to facts that may be empirically verifiable. But in the pre-scientific, ancient world, story was how people knew what was true, who they were, and how they should live in the light of that truth. Story showed them how the divine world interacted with their human world.

1. Lemcio, "Revelation."
2. Denning, "What is story?"

A Story

The Bible comes primarily out of an oral-aural culture, which is one based in speaking and hearing, not primarily in reading and writing. Most of the Bible was written down only after it was spoken and heard. Thus, the Bible's introduction started as an oral communication. It was a story to be heard and passed on, from generation to generation, in the manner of ancient storytellers. It was a truth-story!

When Jesus opened his mouth to teach, he often told stories we call *parables*. In fact, we read, "Jesus told the crowds all these things in parables; without a parable he told them nothing" (Matt. 13:34). So, parables are more than just stories, but stories that open up truth.

"There was a man who had two sons" is the way Jesus began his wonderful parable we usually call "The Prodigal Son" (Luke 15:11–32). Nobody in Jesus' audience worried about whether or not there was literally such a father and his sons. They didn't ask, "Were there really *two* sons? What were their names? Where did they live?" They didn't ask such questions in Jesus' day. Nor do we ask such questions today. Rather, we listen and respond to the powerful story of the loving father, the prodigal son, and the older brother. We may, in fact, recognize ourselves in one of the two brothers in the story.

THE BIBLE'S INTRODUCTION SHOULD BE READ AND UNDERSTOOD AS PART OF THE LITERARY GENRE OF STORY.

In *Retrofuture*, a book about ministering effectively in today's context, author Gerard Kelly observes, "The good news for the Christian faith community is that much of the Bible was story before it was anything else—and that the founder of the faith was without doubt one of history's best

The Story of Beginnings

storytellers. Christian Scripture is rich with living, colorful, multilayered stories to fund our culture's imagination."[3]

In fact, it could be said that all of life is a story. Eugene Peterson puts it this way: "Every day is a story, a morning beginning and evening ending that are boundaries for people who go about their tasks with more or less purpose, go to war, make love, earn a living, scheme and sin and believe. Everything is connected. Meaning is everywhere. The days add up to a life that is a story."[4]

In his recent book, which defines the understanding of gospel in contrast to a more propositional "plan of salvation," New Testament scholar Scot McKnight strongly emphasizes the storied character of what we believe. "The gospel, I am arguing, is declaring the Story of Israel as resolved in the Story of Jesus. . . . [Thus] we dare not permit the gospel to collapse into the abstract, de-storified points in the Plan of Salvation." McKnight continues, "That story is the saving, redeeming, liberating story."[5] His is one of many voices today urging us to recapture the sense of the Bible as story.

Some people are more comfortable with the word *narrative* than with *story*. In their recent book *Origins*, Calvin College scientists Loren and Deborah Haarsma observe that Genesis 1 and 2 "is a narrative, but a carefully constructed one, including rhythm and repetition of ideas."[6]

Genesis is a story—a narrative—of beginnings. As the Bible's introduction, it begins the story of God's involvement with the earth and with human beings, and it sets the stage for telling the larger story. And Genesis 1–3, as the

---

3. Kelly, *Retrofuture*, 101.
4. Peterson, *Answering God*, 47.
5. McKnight, *King Jesus Gospel*, 51–79.
6. Haarsma and Haarsma, *Origins*, 132.

A Story

introduction to Genesis, is itself a story that needs to be told again and again.

The movie *Sarah's Key*, based on the novel by Tatiana De Rosnay, concludes with a striking statement about the impact of story on our lives. "When a story is told it is not forgotten. It becomes a memory of what we were and a hope of what we may become." Genesis 1–3 tells the story of what we were in God's creative intent. It also hints at the larger story of what we may become. This is indeed a story to be told and retold.

ARE THERE TWO CREATION STORIES, OR ONE?

Some see one overall creation story in Genesis 1 and 2. In this view, Genesis 1:1—2:3 is "the overall account of the creation and preparation of the earth as a suitable place for humans to live." Genesis 2:4–25, then, is an "elaboration of the events of the sixth day of Genesis 1."[7]

Others see two stories of creation in Genesis 1 and 2. The first story ends in Genesis 2:3; the second comprises the remainder of chapter 2. These two accounts of the Creator-God's work, like two eyewitness accounts of an incident today, involve variations in detail. But, if we understand these accounts not so much as history and science—as modern people know history and science—but as story conveying basic theological truth, seeming discrepancies between the two stories lose significance. The order of creation and how this account fits into modern science isn't as important as the truth about God conveyed in this story (or stories).

Seattle Pacific University Professor Frank Spina points to a Genesis formula: "this is the generation/story of . . ."

7. Collins, *Adam and Eve*, 52.

This formula is found whenever a new story or genealogy is introduced, including Genesis 2:4, but with the exception of Genesis 1:1. Spina suggests that Genesis 1:1—2:3 tells the basic story of creation, with Genesis 2:4–25 as "the first episode in which God engages the created order."[8]

Continuing into Genesis 3, we move into a segment of the introductory story that we often call *the Fall*, with its consequences felt in human life and in the world as a whole. Indeed, all around us and within us, this Fall story is being played out.

THE BIBLE'S INTRODUCTION ISN'T ONLY A STORY, BUT AN ANCIENT MIDDLE EASTERN STORY.

We may like to think of the Bible's stories as written directly to us. Not so! While the Bible does communicate *with us*, it wasn't originally written *to us*. This story was originally written for ancient Middle Eastern peoples. They were the first to hear and read the Bible's texts, and their culture was dramatically different from ours. Thus, when we read the Bible—more specifically, when we read the Bible's introduction—we must listen not only for the language, but for the culture.

Old Testament scholar John Walton observes of the Bible, "Its message transcends the culture in which it originated, but the form in which the message was imbedded was fully permeated by the ancient culture. . . . Sound interpretation proceeds from the belief that the divine and human authors were competent communicators and that we can therefore comprehend their communication. But to do

---

8. Spina, "The Created Order."

A Story

so, we must respect the integrity of the author by refraining from replacing his message with our own."[9]

In his book *Jesus Through Middle Eastern Eyes*, Kenneth Bailey, a biblical scholar who spent forty years studying and teaching in today's Middle East, provides cultural studies of the different gospels. It makes me wish we had a book titled *Genesis Through Ancient Middle Eastern Eyes*. However, while we may not have a volume with that precise title, we do have an increasing number of careful studies on the ancient Middle Eastern culture within which we must understand Genesis.

Much of today's vision of the Bible's introduction imposes contemporary views of science and history onto Genesis 1–3. But the Bible's introduction isn't from our era; it's from the ancient Middle East. Thus, it must be looked at and listened to with ancient Middle Eastern eyes and ears. If we ignore this reality, we'll miss what the story is really telling us—and we'll do an injustice to the story itself.

RATHER THAN SEE IT PRIMARILY AS ANCIENT STORY, SOME TODAY WANT TO READ GENESIS 1–3 AS A CHAPTER IN HISTORY, AS WE UNDERSTAND HISTORY.

One view of Genesis 1–3 understands it literally, and thus requires that Adam and Eve be literal people who were the first humans on earth. Many today question that understanding of the story and are convinced that scientific evidence points otherwise. Sincere and godly people will end up on both sides of this argument. But is historicity, as modern people understand it, crucial when we consider what kind of literature Genesis 1–3 is? To insist on reading

9. Walton, *Lost World*, 19.

Genesis 1–3 as history defined from a modern point of view is to miss the point of this amazing, ancient story.

Leading evangelical journal *Christianity Today* stated in a June 2011 cover story, "The center of the evolution debate has shifted from asking whether we came from earlier animals to whether we could have come from one man and one woman."[10] In this debate, some evangelical scholars admit to being unconvinced one way or the other. As Tremper Longman III, an Old Testament scholar quoted in the story, acknowledges, "I have not resolved this issue in my own mind except to say that there is nothing that insists on a literal understanding of Adam in a passage [Gen. 1–3] so filled with obvious figurative description."[11]

RATHER THAN SEE IT PRIMARILY AS ANCIENT STORY, SOME TODAY WANT TO READ GENESIS 1–3 AS SCIENTIFIC STATEMENT.

Many read into the creation stories the *how* of God's creation. Genesis 1 and 2, read as a modern, scientific statement, have become ammunition in battles between creationists and evolutionists, and between ways of understanding the *how* of creation. These debates wouldn't have made any sense at all to those who first heard the introduction to the Bible. Today's debates between *intelligent design* and *theistic evolution*, for example, can't be satisfactorily resolved just by quoting verses from Genesis 1 and 2. That's reading back into an ancient text our modern way of thinking—and thus misreading it.

10. Ostling, "Historical Adam," 23.
11. Ibid., 24.

A Story

I SUGGEST THAT WE THINK OF THE CREATION STORY AS HISTORICAL PARABLE.

For the insightful phrase *historical parable*, I'm indebted to Old Testament scholar John Goldingay, a professor at Fuller Theological Seminary. Goldingay writes, "God did not design Genesis 1 to tell us what a camera would have caught if it had been present to film creation. Faulting it for failing to do so misses the point, and defending it to show that it does do so also misses the point."[12] This "missing the point" happens when we insist that science is wrong and the earth was created in six days a few thousand years ago, or when we try to make Genesis fit science by declaring that the days of creation aren't twenty-four-hour days, but longer periods. In fact, "we have no need to try to prove that evolution is untrue or alternatively to try to show that Genesis can be reconciled with it," says Goldingay. "All this means focusing on concerns other than the concerns God had in inspiring this story. Genesis 1 is a portrait, a dramatization, a parabolic story. This does not imply it is not true; it means its truth is expressed in the manner of a parable."[13]

By contrast, John Collins, another contemporary scholar, claims, "If we deny that all people have a common source that was originally good but through which sin came into the world, then the existence of sin becomes God's fault, or even something that God could not avoid." Collins adds that unless we adopt the more literal viewpoint he promotes, "we have given up the grounds, from both the Bible and common sense, for affirming the common dignity of

12. Goldingay, *Genesis for Everyone*, 28.
13. Ibid.

all people, and their common need of the solution that the Biblical faith claims to offer."[14]

I understand the concern to insist on a literal Adam and Eve, fearing that we may dismiss or diminish other parts of the Bible that trouble us. But I don't accept the notion that failure to insist on a literal reading of the Bible's introduction jeopardizes our understanding of sin and salvation, as well as the dignity of human beings. I'm convinced that reading the introduction to the Bible as story or historical parable doesn't negate the reality of sin as rebellion against a loving God, nor our need for reconciliation with God. A subsequent chapter will delve into this key perspective that's introduced in Genesis 3 and unfolded throughout the rest of the Bible. As Professor Goldingay notes, "God brought the first human beings into existence with their vocation, and they turned away from it. That is true whether or not you believe that the theory of evolution helps us understand how God brought them into existence."[15]

Devout believer-scientists Deborah and Loren Haarsma suggest, "If God's purposes in Genesis 1 did not include teaching scientific facts to the Israelites," and the Haarsmas make that case effectively, "then we should not look here for scientific information about the age or development of the world."[16] And Old Testament scholar Peter Enns states, "Christians today misread Genesis when they try to engage it, even minimally, in the scientific arena."[17]

However we understand its details, and on whichever side we find ourselves regarding the argument I've too briefly summarized, the story in the introduction to the Bible is indeed *a true story.* Contemporary historians,

14. Collins, *Adam and Eve*, 134.
15. Goldingay, *Genesis for Everyone*, 63.
16. Haarsma and Haarsma, *Origins*, 143.
17. Enns, *Evolution of Adam*, 33.

A Story

scientists, and theologians may disagree on how far we press the details of the story as we deal with issues of science and history. But we can agree to disagree respectfully while we keep on talking and listening together. The story is true, and it's the basis for what the rest of the Bible teaches about humanity, sin, and salvation.

KEY CHURCH LEADERS AND THEIR NONLITERAL VIEWS OF THE BIBLE'S INTRODUCTION.

Lest we conclude that a nonliteral way of understanding the introduction to the Bible is merely a modern, post-Darwinian way of thinking, it may be helpful to observe that key church leaders prior to the modern age seemed to understand Genesis 1–3 in a nonliteral way. For example, fourth-century church leader Saint Augustine, whose writings are behind much of an orthodox Christian worldview today, thought Genesis 1 and 2 were written according to the understanding of people in ancient times. Augustine wrote, "Perhaps Sacred Scripture in its customary style is speaking with the limitations of human language in addressing men of limited understanding. . . . The narrative of the inspired writer brings the matter down to the capacity of children."[18]

In the sixteenth century, John Calvin wrote in his *Commentaries on the Book of Genesis,* "Nothing is here treated of but the visible form of the world. He who would learn astronomy and the other recondite arts, let him go elsewhere. . . . Moses does not speak with philosophical acuteness on occult mysteries, but states those things which

---

18. Quoted in "Genesis interpreted before Darwin."

are everywhere observed, even by the uncultivated, and which are in common use."[19]

John Wesley, eighteenth-century founder of the Methodist movement, suggested that "the inspired penman in this history [Genesis] . . . [wrote] for the Jews first and, calculating his narratives for the infant state of the church, describes things by their outward sensible appearances, and leaves us, by further discoveries of the divine light, to be led into the understanding of the mysteries couched under them." The scriptures, Wesley also argued, "were written not to gratify our curiosity [of the details] but to lead us to God."[20]

Not long after Darwin published *The Origin of Species* in 1859, Princeton University professor B. B. Warfield, a believer in the inerrancy of Scripture, made this statement: "I am free to say, for myself, that I do not think that there is any general statement in the Bible or any part of the account of creation, either as given Gen. I & II or elsewhere alluded to, that need be opposed to evolution."[21]

The scholar and writer C. S. Lewis has had as much influence on contemporary Christian thought as anyone. Lewis seemed to view the story of Genesis 1–3 in a non-literal way, and to say that whether or not one understands this story literally isn't as important as what the story tells us. In *The Problem of Pain*, Lewis writes:

> For long centuries, God perfected the animal from which was to become the vehicle of humanity and the image of Himself. He gave it hands whose thumb could be applied to each of the fingers, and jaws and teeth and throat capable of articulation. . . . Then, in the fullness of time, God caused to descend upon this

19. Quoted in Haarsma and Haarsma, *Origins*, 144.
20. Quoted in "Genesis interpreted before Darwin."
21. Quoted in Collins and Giberson, *Science and Faith*, 158.

A Story

organism, both on its psychology and physiology, a new kind of consciousness which could say "I" and "me, . . . which knew God, which could make judgments of truth, beauty, and goodness. . . . We do not know how many of these creatures God made, nor how long they continued in the Paradisal state. But sooner or later they fell. Someone or something whispered that they could become as gods. . . . We have no idea in what particular act, or series of acts, the self-contradictory, impossible wish found expression. For all I can see, it might have concerned the literal eating of a fruit, but the question is of no consequence.[22]

IF NONLITERAL WAYS OF LOOKING AT GENESIS 1–3 TROUBLE YOU, PLEASE STAY WITH ME.

I think a nonliteral understanding of the Bible's introduction as a historical parable fits best with scientific and historical evidence. But this book takes the position that a literal or nonliteral view of Genesis 1–3 isn't as important as listening seriously to what this storied introduction to the whole Bible says on its own terms, thereby allowing our lives to be shaped by this fundamental story.

Years ago, I was willing to engage in intense debates about the *how* of creation, first on the literal side and then on the nonliteral side. But I've become increasingly weary of such debates, particularly when they use Genesis 1–3 as ammunition for attack. I've become more and more convinced that such acrimonious arguments often miss the point of this wonderful and storied introduction to the Bible.

22. Lewis, *Problem of Pain*, 72–76.

This doesn't mean that answers to scientific and historical questions aren't important. Nor does this mean that the Bible's introduction has nothing to say regarding scientific and historical questions. But we need to read the Bible as it was intended to be heard and read. I resonate with Loren and Deborah Haarsma, who write, "While Scripture is authoritative and sufficient to teach us everything we need to know to be saved, it is not intended to be a reference book covering all human knowledge.... We wouldn't expect a scientist to use the Bible to figure out how an electronic circuit responds to signals, just as we wouldn't expect a plumber to use the Bible to figure out what size pipe to use in a house under construction."[23] As we pursue science and history, we need to listen to the Bible's main message found in its opening stories and receive it as it was intended to be heard. The truth of the Bible doesn't depend on our ability to fit Genesis 1–3 into a specific scientific or historical framework.

Whether we adopt a literal or a nonliteral way of listening to this story, I hope we'll hear the truth this story is telling us. You may choose to accept a literal interpretation of Genesis 1–3. Regardless, I hope you'll come with me as we open up this powerful, true story and let its light shine on our world and in our personal lives. And I hope you'll come to an increased awareness that the same God described in the Bible's introduction is at work today creating and re-creating that which has fallen.

APPLICATION: LISTEN TO OUR STORY!

Here's my application challenge for this chapter: know and listen to the story of our beginnings. In this ancient story

---

23. Haarsma and Haarsma, *Origins*, 29.

A Story

is our hope for today and tomorrow. The great narrative of "creation—fall—re-creation" is rooted in the Bible's introduction. The saving story of what God has done for us in Jesus begins in the Bible's introduction. And this story, if we tell it often and believe it deeply, shapes and transforms us. We become what our story says we are.

Don't let our story be confused with other framing stories out there in today's world. Listen to what our story says about God, about what God created and intended, and about what God purposes for us and for our world. Go back to this story when confronted with the issues of today. Return regularly to the Bible's introduction and hear this fundamental, life-shaping story. In fact, be like Jesus, who referred questioners back to what God intended "in the beginning." As Scot McKnight says, to come to terms with and effectively communicate this gospel-as-story "we will have to become People of the Story."[24] Live on the basis of our story! Listen to our story!

---

24. McKnight, *King Jesus Gospel*, 1.

3

God

"Who made God?" I asked one of our grandsons, a three-year-old at the time. Of course, this was not a fair question. Raised in a believing family, where the answers for many things involved "Jesus," he replied, "Jesus made God." "Well, who made Jesus?" I asked. "God," was the answer from this budding theologian gifted with circular reasoning. We went on to discuss the heavy-duty concept that nobody made God because God always was and is. At his concrete stage of development, it was hard to grasp that there is a being who wasn't made, and who always was and is.

THE SUBJECT OF THE BIBLE'S FIRST CHAPTER IS GOD.

In the thirty-one verses of Genesis 1, God is referred to at least thirty-five times. The subject of the entire Bible, of its great story, is God. God is the first and chief actor of the entire story. Nothing is more important in the Bible's first chapter than the existence and character of the Creator-God. As

God

Dietrich Bonhoeffer said, "Not the work, no, it is the Creator who is to be glorified."[1] "In the beginning, God . . ."

Sometimes people want to define this first actor with a scientific equation or as a mathematical problem. They reason, "This plus this equals that. If this, then that . . ." But the first actor in the Bible, and the subject of the Bible's first sentence, is God. By definition God can't be fully defined. As Augustine said, "Since it is God we are speaking of, you do not understand it. If you could understand it, it would not be God."[2]

Martin Luther, fifteenth-century reformer, was asked what occupied God before the world's creation. It's reported that Luther responded irritably, "He was cutting switches with which to flog inquisitive questioners."[3]

THE BIBLE'S OPENING WORDS ARE ABOUT HOW GOD EXPRESSED GOD'S SELF IN CREATION.

"In the beginning, God . . ." These opening words of the Bible don't try to prove the existence of God. For the first hearers of these words, "trying to prove God's existence is as odd as trying to prove our own existence."[4] The opening verses of the Bible don't try to prove God's existence, but instead tell a story about how the living God expresses God's self in creation. The Bible's beginning introduces to us the God who has supremely revealed himself to us in Jesus of Nazareth. By the end of the Bible's introduction, we know a lot more about this God, who is there "in the beginning."

1. Bonhoeffer, *Creation and Fall*, 17.
2. Quoted in Wills, *Saint Augustine*, xii.
3. Quoted in Bonhoeffer, *Creation and Fall*, 13.
4. Goldingay, *Genesis for Everyone*, 6.

The Story of Beginnings

As already observed, some readers and commentators today want to treat Genesis 1 as a kind of scientific textbook that tells twenty-first-century people how the world came to be. Genesis 1 is quoted heavily in the ongoing debate regarding evolution versus creation. But these opening words of the whole book's introduction are less about the *how* of creation and more about the *who* of creation.

An aging, New England pastor used to preach once a year on the latest discoveries in astronomy. His younger assistant, anxious to be relevant to people's needs, asked what possible use such a sermon could have. The older man replied, "My dear boy, of course it is no use at all. But it greatly enlarges my idea of God."

Eugene Peterson puts it this way in his insightful introduction to Genesis in *The Message*: "First, God. God is the subject of life. God is foundational for living. If we don't have a sense of the primacy of God, we will never get it right, get life right, get our lives right. Not God at the margins, not God as an option, not God on the weekends. God at center and circumference; God first and last; God, God, God."[5]

To encounter God, we look both into the Bible and at God's creation. Psalm 19 calls us to regard "the heavens [that] declare the glory of God," and attend to "the Law of the Lord, [which] is perfect, reviving the soul" (Ps. 19:1, 7). One of the classic Reformation creeds observes, "We know God by two means: First, by the creation, preservation, and the government of the universe. . . . Second, he makes himself known to us more openly by his holy and divine Word."[6] In this book, our pursuit is to encounter the God who begins the written revelation of God's self in the Bible's introduction.

---

5. Peterson, "Introduction to Genesis."
6. Haarsma and Haarsma, *Origins*, 72.

God

WHAT KIND OF GOD IS INTRODUCED IN THE BIBLE'S INTRODUCTION?

Though the Bible's introduction starts with God as the chief actor in the great story, we need to go beyond that assertion. From this great story, we need to understand *what kind* of God this is. The need to distinguish between accurate and false visions of God—which existed in polytheistic, ancient times when this story was first told—is equally true with contemporary, Western people. Often with us, instead of recognizing that we are created in God's image, we try to create God in our image. God is like us—only bigger and better.

A four-year-old claimed to know exactly what God was like. "Just like my Daddy, only lots bigger!" We took our grandsons to see the movie *Evan Almighty*. In the film, God is portrayed by Morgan Freeman. But should our vision of God be based on that actor? Not long ago, the news reported that it took just three days in prison before a Hollywood starlet found God. Along with the angels in heaven, I rejoice when anyone finds God. But I wonder what kind of god this actress found. A troubled student told a campus chaplain, "I don't believe in God." "Tell me about the God you don't believe in," responded the wise chaplain. When the student described his vision of God, the chaplain said, "I don't believe in that kind of god either!"

WHAT DOES THE BIBLE'S INTRODUCTION TELL US ABOUT THE KIND OF GOD WHO IS ITS SUBJECT?

One word that describes
the God of Genesis 1–3 is *eternal*.

"In the beginning, God . . ." Before anything else was, God was. "From everlasting to everlasting, you are God," is the way the psalmist puts it (Ps. 90:2). Jesus talked about being with God "before the world existed" (John 17:5).

God was there at the beginning of the world and will be there when this world, as we know it, comes to an end. God is there at the beginning of my life, and at the end of my life, and always there in between. Jesus of Nazareth, who fully reveals God, promised his followers, "I am with you always even to the end of the age" (Matt. 28:20). God is eternal and eternally present.

Post–World War II German pastor and theologian Helmut Thielicke says the purpose of the Bible's opening pages is "to show what it means for me and my life that God is there at the beginning and at the end, and that everything that happens in the world—my little life with its cares and its joys, and also the history of the world at large extending from stone-age man to the atomic era—that all this is, so to speak, a discourse enclosed, upheld, and guarded by the breath of God."[7]

Sometimes church leaders have a curious way of referring to a particularly meaningful worship service by saying, "God really showed up!" Of course God showed up! God is always there. The question is whether or not *we* show up. And if we do show up, are we truly present to God? Rather than praying, "Dear God, please show up! Please be with

---

7. Thielicke, *World Began*, 14.

God

us," why not pray, "Dear God, help us to recognize you, worship you, and live in the light of your presence."

From eternity past to eternity to come, God is there. "In the beginning, God..."

Another word to describe the God of Genesis 1–3 is *creative*.

Again and again in this introduction to the Bible, we read, "And God said..." followed by the report of a momentous happening. The psalmist affirms this: "By the word of the Lord the heavens were made, and all their host by the breath of his mouth" (Ps. 33:6). God spoke and it was so!

"Create is a gripping verb in this gripping first line," comments Old Testament scholar John Goldingay, referring to Genesis 1:1.[8] In the Old Testament, only God creates in this way. Of the fifty biblical occurrences of the Hebrew verb *bara* (to create), God is always the subject or implied subject of the verb.[9]

When we think of the word *create*, we usually assume it has to do with bringing something material into existence. Before creation, says Genesis 1:2, "the earth was a formless void." There was nothing! And God made something out of that nothing, out of that chaos. At least, that's the way we often think of creation. But, what if ancient Near Eastern thought understood existence and creation in terms of function, not just material existence? That's the case John Walton, an Old Testament scholar, makes in his book *The Lost World of Genesis One*. "People in the ancient Near East did not think of creation in terms of making material things—instead, everything is function oriented."

8. Goldingay, *Genesis for Everyone*, 6.
9. Walton, *Lost World*, 38.

Walton continues, "In the ancient world, what was most crucial and significant to their understanding of existence was the way that the parts of the cosmos function, not their material status."[10]

This doesn't mean that God isn't responsible for material origins, says Walton. Rather, he affirms that God *is* completely responsible when he writes, "Material origins do involve at some point creation out of nothing."[11] Walton's position has more to do with his attempts to read the account given in Genesis 1 in the light of ancient Middle Eastern thought.

Walton thus proposes an interpretive translation of Genesis 1:1: "In the initial period, God created by assigning functions throughout the heavens and the earth, and this is how he did it."[12] While Walton claims we can't have both material origins and designation of function in Genesis 1, I'm not fully convinced. Thus, I suggest a merging of these two approaches as we consider "In the beginning, God created . . ."

Whatever conclusions we draw about this, Genesis makes it clear that creation wasn't just an accident. What we call creation didn't just happen. It came about because God intended, God spoke, God commanded.

Many scientists describe what they call "random" processes in nature. That is, they refer to an outcome that is unpredictable. But scientists Loren and Deborah Haarsma affirm that such randomness "is entirely compatible with a biblical picture of God's governance. Many Bible passages describe God working through events that appear to be random from a human perspective. . . . Science does nothing to challenge our biblical belief that God governs events

10. Ibid., 26–33.
11. Ibid., 44.
12. Ibid., 45.

God

that appear random from a human perspective."[13] As part of this observation, the Haarsmas cite Proverbs 16:33: "The lot is cast into the lap, but its every decision is from the Lord." Even "random mutation" in evolutionary theory doesn't dismiss God's creative intent to use what seems like random change for God's purpose.

In the creation story, "God said, 'Let there be light' and there was light" (Gen. 1:3). This was before the creation of sun, moon, and stars—heavenly bodies that we understand as "lights." Ancient peoples worshiped these lights as the sun god and the moon god, as divine stars. But in Israel's story, and ours too, God first created the light, which was distinct from darkness. Only then did God, the one true God, create the lights, or luminaries. A scientific question of how there could be light without the lights is irrelevant to the purposes of the story. What the Bible's introduction told its first hearers, and tells us, is that the sun, moon, and stars are not divine. Nor are heavenly bodies able to control human destiny, as is the view of many people today. Rather, the sun, moon, and stars are the handiwork of a creative, light-giving God.

Furthermore, if, as John Walton suggests, ancient people understood creation in terms of function, we may also understand *light* and *darkness* in reference to the time cycle of day and night. Again from Walton: "Time is much more important than the sun—in fact, the sun is not a function, it only has functions. It is a mere functionary."[14] The sun is demoted from deity to functionary.

While we'll think more about the specifics of cosmic creation in the next chapter, let's turn once more to the creation echoes of John's gospel. "In the beginning was the Word, and the Word was with God, and the Word was God" (John 1:1). Regarding this Word of God, the gospel writer

13. Haarsma and Haarsma, *Origins*, 52.
14. Walton, *Lost World*, 55.

continues, "All things came into being through him, and without him not one thing came into being" (John 1:3).

Philip Newell, who writes on Celtic spirituality, says, "Essentially all life is an expression of God. We have been uttered into being." Creation, as Celtic theology tells us, "is the grand volume of God's utterance."[15] This affirmation is not pantheism, despite critiques of Celtic thought by those who are worried about pantheism. Rather, this is God communicating God's very self through the creation.

Another word closely related to the God of the Bible's introduction is *beauty*.

God's creativity expresses power. Along with this power there is beauty, which is another way of expressing the Genesis 1 concept of *goodness*.

"God said, 'Let there be light' and there was light. And God saw that the light was good" (Gen. 1:3–4). Toward the end of the first story, there is an even stronger conclusion: "God saw everything that he had made, and indeed, it was very good" (Gen. 1:31). If ancient people saw creation primarily in terms of functionality, we may have a picture of God joyfully declaring, "It functions well!" Or maybe, "It works beautifully!" Here's another way to put this: "And God saw that it was beautiful, even very beautiful."

So the Bible begins with a word about beauty. Why not? Beauty is characteristic of the God of creation, who celebrates the beauty and goodness of creation. As Helmut Thielicke observes, "The first response the young, dew-fresh creation evoked from the heart of God was joy in its beauty, the rapture of the creator."[16]

15. Newell, *Book of Creation*, xv–xvi.
16. Thielicke, *World Began*, 27.

God

To Job, God describes creation as a time when "the morning stars sang together and all the angels shouted for joy" (Job 38:7). What joy there was over God's beautiful creation, what joy expressing God's own self!

Consider the beauty of *size* and *majesty*. On a scale model, if the earth were drawn one inch away from the sun, Pluto would be three feet away. The star Orion would be five hundred and forty miles away. It's estimated that our galaxy contains one hundred billion stars. And there are at least one hundred billion galaxies in the detectable universe. However it was that God did it—and believing scientists do debate this question—it's God who created it all.

Flying to Fairbanks, Alaska, to visit our son and his family, we glimpsed a few of the one hundred thousand glaciers in Alaska. One glacier alone covers fifteen hundred square miles. There's nothing like pondering vastness and majesty from thirty thousand feet up. As I looked out the little airplane window, I thought, "O God! What an amazing and beautiful and huge and majestic world you created!"

Or think about the blue whale. It's longer than three dump trucks, heavier than one hundred and ten Honda Civics, and has a heart the size of a Volkswagen Beetle. So how much food does it take to sustain such an animal? Try four tons of krill a day—that's three million calories! Even a baby blue whale can put away one hundred gallons of milk every twenty-four hours. When a blue whale surfaces, it takes in the largest breath of air of any living thing on the planet. And its spray shoots higher into the air than the height of a telephone pole.

The psalmist sings about Leviathan, which God created "to sport" in the sea (Ps. 104:26). Maybe Leviathan was some kind of sea dragon. Or maybe it was a blue whale. Whatever Leviathan was, it was a part of God's majestic creation.

On a flight between Seattle and Boise, Idaho, I meditated on the tremendous variety of the landscape below.

The Story of Beginnings

Some stretches of land looked like it had been folded and crinkled. Jagged mountains reached toward the sky. Desert-like expanses gave way to forests. I thought, "Yes, God, you are creator of all I see from the vantage point of twenty-five thousand feet. But you didn't throw these things down in this seemingly random fashion. Instead, there were natural forces that, over time, folded some of the earth's surface. Other powerful forces, again over time, pushed up craggy mountains and dug deep valleys. You are the Creator-God. But it seems obvious that you used these powerful natural forces to shape your creation."

Then, I wondered why it's not just as reasonable that God allowed natural forces over time to shape and change living creatures—animals and humans. Why must evolution always be a bad word to some believers, especially when evolution is observed by people who understand and believe in God as creator? Why must our heated debates over evolution and creationism muddy the waters of our understanding that God is the majestic creator of all that is?

Consider also the beauty of *color* and *shape*. Kayaking and snorkeling in Makena Bay at the south end of Maui, we came close, but not too close, to giant sea turtles. We watched a diverse mix of brilliantly colored fish in coral reefs. And we were treated to a stunning sunset. But I don't have to go to Hawaii to celebrate the arresting beauty of God's creation. Have you noticed a baby's fingers, all ten of them tiny and perfectly formed? Do we pause to marvel at the beauty of a baby's fingers?

Because the Creator-God is a lover of beauty, we human beings are gifted with the ability to shape beautiful things and make beautiful music. Listen to music and look at a piece of art and celebrate the God who gifts human beings with creativity. Yet there's more to beauty than art and music. Mother Teresa made it her life's work to do

God

something beautiful for God. And she did so by caring for the poor and dying of Calcutta, India, in whom she saw the beauty of their Creator-God.

I once listened to a bright, attractive college girl complain bitterly that she hadn't seen anything in Christianity that appealed to her sense of beauty and color. Why should she surrender to being cramped and narrow and ugly and dull? I tried to point out that even though some of God's servants ended up with small and negative views of life, it wasn't what God intended. When we as human beings are narrow and ugly, we don't reflect God; rather, we're a distortion of what God intended us to be. In chapter 4, we'll think about how God intends for us to reflect and express God's own beautiful image and likeness.

Again and again, in the first chapter of the Bible, we hear the refrain, "And God saw that it was good . . ." Read: "And God saw that it was beautiful!"

One more word that describes the God of Genesis 1 is *personality*.

The God of the Bible's introduction isn't an "it," or merely a "force," or a "wholly other." This God is a "thou," a *Being* with personality, and one who loves and desires to be loved. The God of the Bible and our God today is not a cosmic engineer, who merely set the universe in motion, then ceased involvement with it. This God is infinite and personal. As the psalmist sings to God,

> Once God has spoken,
> Twice have I heard this:
> That power belongs to God,
> And steadfast love belongs to you, O Lord.
> (Ps. 62:11–12)

The Story of Beginnings

The God of the Bible's beginning is not only powerful enough to create the cosmos, but also is loving and covenant keeping. This God of creation desires not only obedience from his human creatures, but also relationship. This personal God is relational.

The God of Genesis 2 is grieved that the human should be alone. This *aloneness,* which we'll discuss further in the chapter "God Created Humans for Love," is the only thing in God's creation declared to be "not good" (Gen. 2:18). God created human beings for relationship and partnership with God's own self and with other beings like them. So, as we shall see moving through this story, God creates a partner for the human—a partner like him, yet different, and with whom he would live in covenant relationship.

The God of Genesis 3 is a Lover-God, who lays out boundaries for the good of the first humans. This God is an offended lover when Adam and Eve disregard those boundaries. This offended lover comes searching for the man and the woman, who have now hidden from their Creator-God, and calls out to them. But God doesn't angrily shout out, "What have you done?" Rather, God calls out, "Where are you?" (Gen. 3:9). This isn't a cry of angry judgment, but of grief-stricken love. The offended Lover-God wants to know why the loved ones are hiding from him.

This personal God loved and loves the world God created, especially the human beings created in God's own image. Imagine: This is the God who commanded a world into being, and one hundred billion other planets in our galaxy, and one hundred billion other galaxies. This is the God who formed the intricacies of the human body, including that marvelous computer, the brain. And this God loves me, this five-foot ten-inch organism, one of about seven billion inhabitants of this comparatively insignificant spinning ball out there in the cosmos. Saint Augustine is reported to have

God

declared, "God loves each of us as if there was only one of us to love." What a wonder!

"In the beginning, God . . ." This is the first and primary actor in the story and in its introduction. As scientist-theologian David Wilkinson has observed, "We need to be very careful about focusing on the Creator—not on just creation."[17]

WHEN WE WANT TO KNOW WHAT THIS CREATOR-GOD IS LIKE, WE LOOK AT JESUS.

This first actor, this main character, revealed himself to the creation in the form of a human being. As John 1 puts it, with its echoes of creation, "No one has ever seen God. It is God the only Son, who is close to the Father's heart, who has made him known" (John 1:18).

As Paul taught the church in Colossae, Jesus expresses the fullness of who God is and what God is like. "He [Jesus] is the image of the invisible God . . . ; for in him all things in heaven and on earth were created" (Col. 1:15–16). Jesus, the Son, was there at the creation as the opening verses of Hebrews also affirm: "In these last days God has spoken to us by the Son, whom he appointed heir of all things, through whom he also created the world." This Son, says Hebrews, "is the reflection of God's glory and the exact imprint of God's very being" (Heb. 1:1–3).

Jesus, the Son, expresses the Creator-God, the first actor and the main character in the Bible's great story. And it's the ongoing purpose of God to re-create in us God's own likeness as expressed fully in Jesus. We're not left merely with the failure of our first parents and the sad consequences of that failure. As we'll observe more fully in the

17. Wilkinson, "Bigger," 28.

final chapter of this book, in the midst of those sad consequences there's the hope-filled divine purpose to transform us and to transform the whole world into something new and beautiful and loving.

APPLICATION: THE MOST APPROPRIATE HUMAN RESPONSE TO THE GOD OF BEGINNINGS IS WORSHIP.

In her book *In the Beginning, God*, theologian Marva Dawn urges, "As we look closely at Genesis 1–3, let us keep constantly in mind that the issue is worship. Many people who read this passage fail to keep this issue central and therefore ask the wrong questions, for the biblical accounts of the Creation and the Fall are not meant to be a science textbook." Dawn continues to urge worship as the outcome of listening to the Bible's introduction: "When you see the wonders of the earth and sky, don't you respond with greater gratitude to their Creator, increased praise to God?"[18]

After a detailed analysis of various views among believers about creation, evolution, and intelligent design, Deborah and Loren Haarsma close their book *Origins* with an excellent chapter on "Wonder and Worship." They point out that "in the church today heated debates over origins and other science issues can detract from worship and praise. Christians hear pastors or Christian radio stations saying that scientists are trying to disprove God, or that scientific advances will challenge their faith." The Haarsmas conclude, "But when the church's response to science is dominated by debate, it can leave the negative impression that science is all about controversy, challenges, and divisions among Christians. Thus, it is important for churches

18. Dawn, *In the Beginning*, 17.

to make a special effort to praise God for what science has discovered about God's world."[19]

Mary Susanne Edgar, a Canadian who lived from 1889 to 1973, was involved in YWCA work, helping to establish Camp Glen Barnard for Girls in northern Ontario. Edgar's poetic words for campers won first prize in a contest conducted by the American Camping Association. Set to a tune by Harold Lowden, Edgar's creation-celebrating poem is sometimes sung as a hymn. Let these words lead us into worship of our Creator-God.

> God who touches earth with beauty, make my heart anew.
> With your Spirit recreate me, pure and strong and true.
> Like your springs and running waters, make me crystal pure.
> Like your rocks of tow'ring grandeur make me strong and sure.
> Like your dancing waves in sunlight, make me glad and free.
> Like the straightness of the pine trees, let me upright be.
> Like the arching of the heavens, lift my thoughts above.
> Turn my dreams to noble actions, ministries of love.[20]

---

19. Haarsma and Haarsma, *Origins*, 289.
20. Tindal and Middleton, *Songs*, #76.

4

God Created

> O Lord, how manifold are your works!
> In wisdom you have made them all . . . ;
> When you send forth your spirit, they are created;
> And you renew the face of the earth.
> (Ps. 104:24, 30)

PSALMISTS SING PRAISES REGARDING the varied and wonderful "works of the Lord." Psalm 104 in particular celebrates the Creator-God, who is "clothed with honor and majesty, wrapped in light as with a garment." The psalm continues, "You stretch out the heavens like a tent, . . . make the clouds a chariot, you ride on the wings of the wind" (Ps. 104:1–4). Later the psalmist exclaims to the Creator-God, "You make springs gush forth in the valleys; . . . You cause grass to grow for the cattle, and plants for people to use" (Ps. 104:10, 14).

In the book of Revelation, the Bible's conclusion to its great story, heavenly beings celebrate God as creator:

> You are worthy, our Lord and God,
> To receive glory and honor and power,

God Created

> For you created all things,
> And by your will they existed and were created.
> (Rev. 4:11)

And in the climax to Revelation, yet to be experienced by us, is the creation of "a new heaven and a new earth" (Rev. 21:1).

In the Bible's introduction, the first creation story from Genesis 1 isn't concerned with *how* God did it. The storyteller simply affirms that "God spoke . . ." and it was so. The *who* and the *what* of creation are celebrated from beginning to end in the Bible.

Irish monk Columbanus said, "If you wish to know the Creator, come to know his creatures."[1] Significantly, this Celtic missionary founded a monastery in Italy, where Saint Francis of Assisi was trained. Few, if any, in the church's history have celebrated God's creation more than Saint Francis.

A PARABLE OF MICE IN A PIANO.

When I think of God and creation, my mind turns to another story, an old parable I heard once. This parable of mice in a piano puts some of the issues of creation in perspective.

> Imagine a family of mice who lived all their lives in a large, old, upright piano. Into their piano world comes the music of the instrument, filling dark spaces with sound and harmony. The mice are impressed by the music and draw comfort and wonder from the thought that there is this Someone who makes the music, invisible to them, above them, yet close to them. They love to think of the great Piano Player whom they cannot see. But one day, a daring mouse climbs up part of the piano and returns thoughtful,

1. Quoted in Newell, *Book of Creation*, 68.

The Story of Beginnings

> claiming to have discovered how the music is made. "Why," he reports, "wires are the secret, tightly stretched wires, wires of graduated lengths, wires which tremble and vibrate." And this explorer mouse proclaims the theory of the wires to explain the origin of music that fills the piano. Another explorer mouse carries the explanation further. Hammers are the secret, he discovers. There are hammers dancing and leaping on the wires. And he proclaims the theory of the hammers to explain the piano music's origin. Many of the mice now begin to think the music is purely mechanical in origin. They begin to assume that the unseen Piano Player is just a myth. But the music continues, the musician playing the piano, regardless of what the mice think about the music's origin.

In this parable, the great, unseen Player isn't the same as the piano. Many today confuse the piano player, the piano, and the mice, believing they're all of the same essence. Not so, according to the story of Genesis 1! God is God, and the creation is separate from God. Ancient paganism saw God and nature as one. Modern paganism sees God and "Mother Earth" as one. We call this *pantheism*.

Many today, if they believe in an unseen Player, think he, she, or it is distant, unconnected, uninvolved with the music, almost like a player piano, mechanically producing the sound. We call this *deism*. Again, not so, says the introduction to the Bible! The God of creation, as we observed in the last chapter, is a personal God—is, in fact, the God who personally revealed himself in Jesus. Despite what the mice begin to think, the unseen Piano Player is personally involved with the music, a creator who tenderly touches the keys, which activate little hammers, which strike the wires, which produce beautiful and meaningful sounds. Indeed, it's the music that expresses who the musician is!

Some people picture an unseen Piano Player who is irrational, even vengeful, venting unpredictable emotions on the piano, producing sounds that can hardly be called musical. Imagine the little mice inside the piano, buffeted by this noise, sometimes afraid of the unseen Player. "What did we do to deserve this?" they might ask one another. Once again, not so! The unseen Player—the God of the Bible's introduction—is a consistent being, characterized by holiness and love. True, at times the music is uncomfortable, dissonant, and troubling to the mice. But music that seems harsh, and which the mice can't always understand, is really part of a larger whole that contains profound beauty. Dissonance can resolve into harmony. But even if it doesn't, there's power and beauty in the dissonance.

AMONG NON-ISRAELITE, ANCIENT MIDDLE EASTERN PEOPLE, THERE WERE OTHER STORIES OF CREATION IN ADDITION TO THE STORIES OF GENESIS 1 AND 2.

Other ancient Middle Eastern stories seem to overlap with the Genesis story. Their influence is also felt elsewhere in the Old Testament. For example, Leviathan, a sea monster that appears in ancient Middle Eastern epics, is cited in Psalm 74:14: "You crushed the heads of Leviathan; you gave him as food for the creatures of the wilderness." Leviathan also appears in Isaiah 27:1: "On that day the Lord . . . will punish Leviathan the fleeing serpent, Leviathan the twisting serpent, and he will kill the dragon that is in the sea."

But the differences between Israel's story and other ancient stories are more striking than their similarities.

The Story of Beginnings

As Fuller professor John Goldingay puts it, "If anything, Genesis was setting itself over against those other accounts of creation: 'You know what your neighbors say about creation? Well now I will tell you the real truth.'"[2] Other creation stories involved multiple gods who, as the source of creation, either cooperated with or were in conflict with one another. These other creation stories talked about the gods themselves coming into existence. But Genesis points clearly to one God, the uncreated Creator-God. Thus, this storied introduction to the Bible contains "a polemic element that contrasts Israel's God with the polytheistic creation and flood stories of the ancient Mesopotamian world in which Hebrews lived. . . . The text was written in a way that would show stark contrast to the established belief systems that surrounded the Hebrews."[3]

THE GENESIS STORY OF CREATION BEGINS IN CHAOS.

The Hebrew words *tohu* and *bohu* in Genesis 1:2 speak of formlessness and emptiness. "The earth was a formless void and darkness covered the face of the deep," or, "The earth was without shape or form," as rendered by the Common English Bible. "And the earth—it was a desert and a wasteland" is the way commentator Victor Hamilton translates it.[4] Or as Eugene Peterson's creative paraphrase in *The Message* puts it, "Earth was a soup of nothingness, a bottomless emptiness."

Jewish author Leon Kass observes, "We may be disappointed in the text's lack of clarity, but we are at the same

2. Goldingay, *Genesis for Everyone*, 7.
3. "How to approach scripture."
4. Hamilton, *Book of Genesis*, 208.

God Created

time grateful that the account leaves mysterious what cannot help but be mysterious."[5]

However we render the words and understand the story's meaning, we get the picture of a disordered and nonfunctional chaos. Out of this the Creator-God brings order through the action of God's breath, or spirit: "A wind [or spirit] from God swept over the face of the waters" (Gen. 1:2).

But chaos doesn't just describe what existed before God began to create. It also speaks of subsequent eras of human life, and of times that seem particularly empty of meaning and order. Even in recent human history, moments of chaos abound, moments that lead to distressed proclamations, such as when Mahatma Gandhi's assassination led India's Prime Minister Jawaharlal Nehru to declare, "The light has gone out of our lives and there is darkness everywhere."

As we observed earlier, many scholars think Genesis was written down and read during the Babylonian exile. People in exile would've seen their lives as full of darkness and not fully functioning. However, the creation story in the Bible's introduction would've reminded the people of Israel during the darkness of Babylonian exile that God can transform such a dire and dismal, light-has-gone-out situation. Transformation from empty waste to ordered cosmos is what the Creator-God does! "The earth was a formless void and darkness covered the face of the deep, while a wind from God swept over the face of the waters. Then God said, 'Let there be light; and there was light'" (Gen. 1:2–3).

---

5. Kass, *Beginning of Wisdom*, 29.

The Story of Beginnings

THE BIBLE'S INTRODUCTION TELLS OF PROGRESSIVE ORDER OUT OF CHAOS.

On the first day of creation, or what we might call "Sunday," there is light that comes at God's word. It's like God turns the lights on at the beginning of a progression from chaos to order. John's gospel tells us, "In him was light and the light was the light of all people. The light shines in the darkness, and the darkness did not overcome it" (John 1:4–5). As Philip Newell observes, "To say that light is created on the first day is to say that light is at the heart of life. It is the beginning of creation in the sense that it is the essence or centre from which life proceeds."[6]

On the second day of creation, or "Monday," there's sea and sky, which come at God's word. The storyteller speaks of "a dome in the middle of the waters to separate the waters from each other. . . . God named the dome Sky" (Gen. 1:6–8, CEB). Look up at the sky and see if it doesn't look almost like a cosmic dome! Clearly this is storytelling, not science as we understand science.

If we think in terms of function, God is establishing the functions that serve as the basis for weather—that is, the waters above and the waters below. Read it in the direct and pointed language of *The Message*:

> God spoke: "Sky! In the middle of the waters;
> separate water from water!"
> God made sky.
> He separated the water under sky
> from the water above sky. . . .
> He named sky the Heavens; . . .
> God spoke: "Separate!
> Water-beneath-Heaven, gather into one place;
> Land, appear!"

---

6. Newell, *Book of Creation*, 3.

God Created

And there it was.
God named the land Earth.
He named the pooled water Ocean."

On the third day, or "Tuesday," after creating seas and sky, God creates earth—"Land!"—followed by the creation of vegetation on "the dry land Earth." "Plants yielding seed, and fruit trees of every kind on earth that bear fruit with the seed in it" all came into being or were assigned their appropriate function at God's word (Gen. 1:11). This is God creating the basis for food: plants, vegetation, fruit trees. This proliferation of plant life was orderly and consistent. Each plant and fruit had within it the seed to bear its own kind, not something totally different. Apples produce apples, not asparagus!

Yes, there are ways in which the creation, at least what we see of it today, seems disordered and diseased. But people like the Celts, both ancient and modern, view the world and life through "the garden lens" (referring to the Garden of Eden), which celebrates "the goodness that is deeper than evil."[7]

In the chapter "God," I referred you to scholarship by John Walton, who focuses on a functional rather than material-origins understanding of Genesis 1. This approach leads Walton to read, "On day one God created the basis for time; day two the basis for weather; and day three the basis for food. These three great functions—time, weather, and food—are the foundations of life."[8] I invite us to hear both: that God creates in a material sense and assigns functions/roles.

On "Wednesday," or creation's fourth day, God's word brings into being not the light, but the "lights": two great lights, one for the day and the other for the night. Then,

7. Newell, *Book of Creation*, 37.
8. Walton, *Lost World*, 58.

almost as an afterthought, along with the sun and moon, God's word brings forth stars.

As already observed, one way to understand the dating of the Bible's introduction is to see it as coming from the period of Babylonian exile in the sixth century before Christ. Babylonians consulted heavenly bodies when they wanted to know what the gods were doing and what was going to happen. So, while in Babylonian exile with this kind of influence surrounding them, the Bible's introduction reminded Israel that its one true God was in charge of these heavenly bodies. As the prophet Isaiah declared, "Lift up your eyes on high and see: Who created these? He who brings out their host and numbers them, calling them all by name; because he is great in strength, mighty in power, not one is missing" (Isa. 40:26). John Goldingay puts it this way: "They are not gods or representatives of gods; the sun and moon are just lampposts in the sky. This subtly puts sun and moon and stars in their place."[9]

On "Thursday," or the fifth day, God's word brings about the multitude of "living creatures." In the waters, in the sky, on the earth were "great sea monsters" and "every winged bird of every kind" (Gen. 1:21). "Sea monsters" were particularly ominous creatures to non-Israelite people. To the Canaanites, these sea monsters were enemies and opponents of the great god Baal. To Babylonians, the sea monster Tiamet existed even before the gods. But "no doubt is left by this chapter that the most fearsome of creatures were from God's good hand. There may be rebels in his kingdom, but no rivals."[10] Once again, there is the repetition "And God said . . . And it was so . . . And God saw that it was good" (Gen. 1:20–21).

---

9. Goldingay, *Genesis for Everyone*, 7.
10. Kidner, *Genesis*, 49.

God Created

When we come to the sixth day of creation, to "Friday," we begin with creatures of the earth. God spoke and there came into being "cattle and creeping things and wild animals of the earth of every kind" (Gen. 1:24). The living creatures of the earth seem to fit into three classes. There are cattle, which are associated particularly with the human creation to follow. Next, there are creeping things, creatures that move on the ground as opposed to being in the air or sea. These may include reptiles, insects, and mice. Then there are "wild animals of the earth of every kind." These creatures fit into orderly categories, just as the rest of the creation. And over all is the blessing, "And God saw that it was good" (Gen. 1:25).

At about "Friday noon" in the creation, I imagine a pause in the story. You get the sense that the Creator-God is contemplating the momentous character of the next creative act. God seems to deliberate within God's own self: "Then God said, 'Let us make humankind . . .'" (Gen. 1:26). We'll cover human creation and the assigning of an appropriate function to humans—the pinnacle of creation—in the next chapter.

> "God looked over everything he had made;
> It was so good, so very good!
> It was evening, it was morning—
> Day Six." (*The Message*)

"In the beginning, when God created . . ." (Gen. 1:1) says the Bible's introduction. However we understand *how* the creator did it, we can confidently affirm this *who* of creation, the God who is the subject of this storied introduction. The progress from chaos to order, which I've related above, is in biblical terms, not scientific. Again, we look to the Bible's introduction not for scientific or historical data, but for a story that gives meaning to what we see around us. Believers, regardless of the scientific explanations given for creation, affirm that it's God who created. As Leon Kass notes, "Darwin himself was utterly baffled by how life first arose; in the last words of the last edition of *Origin of Species*, he repairs to 'the Creator' as the ultimate source of the first breath of life."[11]

APPLICATION: WONDER!

The most appropriate human response to creation isn't analysis, but wonder. This is the application I urge us to engage in after considering God as cosmic creator.

I recently suggested to our three-year-old granddaughter that we take her tricycle outside. "Yes!" she said. "Let's go out and see the world!" When I mentioned that maybe we'd gone far enough up the sidewalk, she complained, "But I want to see more of the world!" Later that day at the zoo, she talked excitedly about seeing the world. In her voice was the wonder of childhood, so easily lost by adults.

More important than trying to figure it out or attempting to fit creation neatly into a scientific theory, our response is more appropriately, "O God, what a wonder you are! What a wonderful creator you are!" Questions of science and history are valid. We can and should ask them. But questions of analysis shouldn't outdo the response of wonder, which is what is intended by the Bible's introduction.

The often misunderstood and maligned Celtic teacher Pelagius pointed to what he called "the good of nature and the good of grace."[12] Both call us to a creation vision, and to the response of wonder. Homiletics professor Zack Eswine urges preachers to use "the garden lens" when describing

11. Kass, *Beginning of Wisdom*, 51.
12. Quoted in Newell, *Book of Creation*, 40.

God Created

our world and God's intention for it. This lifts our gaze merely from the sordid and sinful vision often preoccupying our worldview. Writes Eswine, "When someone hears a biblical sermon, they are meant to declare with the beavers from Narnia 'They say Aslan is on the move.'" Eswine is referencing author C. S. Lewis's wonderful parable, *The Chronicles of Narnia*, where "when Aslan is on the move, ice melts, the earth warms, and Christmas returns."[13]

One summer, from the vantage point of fifty-five hundred feet at Hurricane Ridge in western Washington's Olympic National Park, my wife and I marveled at the quiet majesty of the inner Olympic Mountains. The scene refused to be captured within the confines of a photograph, and it stirred my heart to wonder. Later, from thirty thousand feet, I viewed again the stunning landscape of the Cascade Mountains breaking through the "marine layer," which often blankets the earth in my part of the world. Am I curious about how the Cascades and the Olympics came into being? Of course! And geologists have their explanations. But as a believer, I'm drawn not just to analysis, but also to wonder and worship of the Creator-God.

The psalmists lead us in wonder-filled responses. I suggest that we take our cue from these ancients songwriters.

> Make a joyful noise to God, all the earth;
> Sing the glory of his name,
> Give to him glorious praise.
> Say to God, "How awesome are your deeds!"
> (Ps. 66:1)

> The heavens are telling the glory of God,
> And the firmament proclaims his handiwork.
> (Ps. 19:1)

---

13. Eswine, *Post-Everything World*, 42.

The Story of Beginnings

> O Lord, our Sovereign,
> How majestic is your name in all the earth!
> You have set your glory above the heavens.
> (Ps. 8:1)

> Praise him, sun and moon;
> Praise him, all you shining stars!
> Praise him, you highest heavens,
> And you waters above the heavens!
> Let them praise the name of the Lord,
> For he commanded and they were created.
> (Ps. 148:3–5)

5

God Created Image Bearers

"The human being," I've heard it observed, "walks down a lonely road between two hospitals. He is born in one and dies in another." And somewhere along that road we pause and ask some questions: "Who am I? Where have I come from? What am I doing here?" These are key questions dealt with in the Bible's introduction.

Decades ago, popular author Francis Schaeffer wrote, "People today are trying to hang on to the dignity of man and they do not know how to because they have lost the truth that we are made in the image of God."[1] True in Schaeffer's day—and true today! A key emphasis of the Bible's introduction is the creation of human beings in God's image. It's by understanding and living in the light of God's image—the imago dei—that we deal with the questions of who we are, where we came from, and what we're doing on earth.

"In the beginning, God created . . ." says the first verse of the Bible. From there until verse 26 of Genesis 1, the story

---

1. Schaeffer, *Escape From Reason*, 24.

follows a predictable progression: "God said . . . God created . . . God made . . ." and "It was the third day . . . fourth day . . . fifth day . . ." Then I imagine that God—after creating the world of nature and assigning all of creation its functions and roles—paused as if to contemplate the huge significance of what God was about to do. For in this ancient story, God was about to create the pinnacle of creation: the human being.

In the second creation story (Gen. 2:4–25), we hear that God "formed man [*adam*] from the dust of the ground [*adamah*] and breathed into his nostrils the breath of life, and the man became a living being" (Gen. 2:7). This isn't "a living soul" as rendered by the King James Version, but a "living being." The Bible's introduction doesn't divide us into body and soul, as Western Christians tend to do. Rather, as Professor John Goldingay says, "it is a whole person that we are created and as a whole person that we will be raised to resurrection life."[2] So here is the human being related to the ground, but inbreathed by God to become "a living being."

The New Revised Standard Version doesn't use the name "Adam" to apply to this human creature until Genesis 5:2: "This is the list of the descendants of Adam . . ." Until then, the NRSV speaks of "the man," referencing Adam in a footnote. The New International Version first applies Adam as a name in Genesis 2:20: "But for Adam no suitable helper was found." Why the ambiguity? The Hebrew word *adam* doesn't refer specifically to a male creature, but is the generic term for "earth creature," which comes from *adamah*, or "ground." God makes *adam* as both male and female.

So how shall we understand this earth creature? How shall we understand the human being scientifically? I've made the case that Genesis 1–3 isn't to be combed in search

2. Goldingay, *Genesis for Everyone*, 32.

God Created Image Bearers

of scientific data. Yet wondering who humans are and where we came from raises scientific questions. Dealing with the human being places us at an important intersection between Scripture and science.

THE INTERSECTION OF SCRIPTURE AND SCIENCE GENERATES SEVERAL SCENARIOS.

Each of these proposals about the origins of humanity has theological and scientific problems, which I won't discuss at length. For a good summary of the options, I refer you to *Origins* by Deborah and Loren Haarsma. As scientists and believers, the couple says none of the proposed scenarios are completely satisfying. But the Haarsmas encourage thoughtful believers to continue to study and work in this area.

The following summarizes the views offered by these two scientists:[3]

1. Adam and Eve were recent ancestors, the first humans, who were specially created by God around ten thousand years ago. This is the most traditional view, and it's the scenario that may be the most difficult to reconcile with science.

2. Adam and Eve were recent representatives, a pair selected by God from among other humans about ten thousand years ago. But the wider pool of humanity was created some one hundred fifty thousand years ago.

3. Adam and Eve were ancient ancestors, a pair of hominids who had developed through evolutionary mechanisms approximately one hundred fifty thousand

---

3. Haarsma and Haarsma, *Origins*, 254–71.

years ago. God selected this pair and miraculously modified them into the first humans.

4. Adam and Eve were a group of humans who came into being through evolutionary creation about one hundred fifty thousand years ago. There were other humans alive at the time, but this group was chosen by God to represent the rest of humanity.

5. Adam and Eve are symbolic of the human race, which came into being through evolutionary creation some one hundred fifty thousand years ago.

"Remember," urge the Haarsmas, "that proponents of each view can be working in good faith to reconcile God's revelations in Scripture and in nature and to maintain certain central theological beliefs."[4]

WE WERE CREATED IN THE IMAGE OF GOD.

Returning to the story line of Genesis 1, notice words that are absolutely crucial for understanding who we are and what we're to be about: "Let us make the human being in our image, according to our likeness" (Gen. 1:26). In *Origins*, Loren and Deborah Haarsma observe, "Even if humans share a common ancestry with apes and other animals, our line of descent diverged from that of other animals at some point. Something different happened in our line of descent that makes us unique among life-forms on earth. Our significance . . . lies not primarily in our biological uniqueness but in how God chooses to relate to us." In other words, God chose to reveal himself to human beings, to be in relationship with human beings, and to give human beings a commission not given to other living creatures.[5]

4. Ibid., 270.
5. Ibid., 279.

God Created Image Bearers

We're created in the image of God. Regardless, therefore, of how pessimistic we are about the state of humanity and human society today, you and I still reflect—however dimly or partially—the image of God. *That* is the heart of our identity, the core of who we are. And that should be the essence of our answers to the question "Who am I?" After all, I'm not primarily a sinner, as most basically defined by the tragic story told in Genesis 3. Nor am I most basically heterosexual or homosexual, American or Chinese, Methodist or Presbyterian, Republican or Democrat. No, I'm fundamentally a person created in the image of God!

WHAT DOES THIS "IMAGE OF GOD" MEAN?

Some theologians have talked about the image of God almost as if it were some *thing*. Some have made lists of God-qualities seen in human beings, including conscience, the soul, original righteousness, reason, and a capacity for fellowship with God through prayer.[6]

Old Testament scholar Peter Enns insists that on the basis of ancient Near Eastern studies and Old Testament evidences, we should limit our understanding of the image of God to "humanity's role as ruler over creation, as God's earthly representatives. . . . Humans were God's images to represent to all creatures God's rule over the earth."[7] While this theory is intriguing, why limit our understanding of imago dei to this one function?

Another intriguing way to look at the image of God is to see the whole of creation as a kind of temple, or dwelling, for God. In ancient temples, there was an image or statue of the god to whom the temple was dedicated. In Israel,

6. Hamilton, *Book of Genesis*, 137.
7. Enns, *Evolution of Adam*, xv.

of course, there wouldn't be this kind of image of God. Instead, the "human image of God" was placed in God's creation-temple to reflect God.

I suggest that the most basic way to understand the image of God is to do so relationally. We're God's earthly representatives, yes, but we're also created to be in relationship with God, who is Father, Son, and Spirit. The imago dei involves the way we relate to and reflect God. As British scholar David Wilkinson puts it, "Bearing God's image is about *relationship* with God more than any specific human attribute or pattern of behavior."[8]

But practically speaking, what does this mean?

THE IMAGE OF GOD SPEAKS OF OUR DIGNITY.

There's a clear distinction in the Bible's introduction between material, plant, and animal worlds on one hand and the human world on the other. It's only into human nostrils that God breathed the breath of life, says the story in Genesis 2:7. As the pinnacle of God's creation, human beings are the ultimate self-expression of God. Recognizing that "the place and special dignity of man is today on the defensive," Jewish scholar and author Leon Kass writes, "Human beings really are different from and higher than the other animals, and only the human animal could be called godlike."[9] The uniqueness of humanity due to our creation in God's image is something we mustn't lose sight of.

In ancient Egyptian and Mesopotamian society, a king or other high-ranking person might be called "the image of God." But such a designation was never applied to a common laborer. The Bible's introduction was unique in the

8. Wilkinson, "Bigger," 29.
9. Kass, *Beginning of Wisdom*, 37.

God Created Image Bearers

ancient world because it describes all humans as being "in the image of God." As Old Testament commentator Victor Hamilton puts it, "All of humanity is related to God, not just the king. Specifically, the Bible democratizes the royalistic and exclusivistic concept of the nations that surrounded Israel."[10] We're *all* God's representatives in God's world.

Several years ago, I was waiting at a stoplight. In the car ahead of me a young man was tenderly stroking the hair of a platinum blond seated beside him. He was caressing, stroking, scratching, and even getting his face down into this lovely head of hair. I thought, "How sweet! How tender and romantic. Isn't this nice?" But then the head turned and I saw it was a big white dog in the passenger seat! Now, dogs can be man's or woman's best friend. But even a platinum-blond dog can't match a human being.

Revelation 4 pictures all of creation's response to the "one seated on the throne" (Rev. 4:2), including four living creatures: one like a lion, one like an ox, one like a human, and one like an eagle. They all offer worship to the one on the throne. But it's uniquely the human worshipers represented in the twenty-four elders who know *why* they worship: "You are worthy, our Lord and God . . . for you created all things" (Rev. 4:11). In his commentary on Revelation, N.T. Wright observes, "Creation as a whole simply worships God; the humans who represent God's people *understand why they do so*. . . . Humans are given the capacity to reflect, to understand what's going on. And, in particular, to express that understanding in worship."[11] That capacity to worship with understanding is part of our image-of-God-based dignity.

If we're committed to the dignity of all human beings, do we treat one another as those who reflect the image of

10. Hamilton, *Book of Genesis*, 135.
11. Wright, *Revelation for Everyone*, 48.

God? Rich Mouw of Fuller Theological Seminary urges, "God wants us to offer a fundamental respect to others purely on the basis of their humanness. Christians and Muslims, African Americans and Jewish Americans, heterosexuals and homosexuals, rich and poor—all are created in the divine likeness."[12]

As a believer in creation, I'm to treat all other members of the human race with respect, regardless of color, race, personal habits, and behaviors. Imagine the impact in this anger-and-hate-charged world if Christ-followers lived out their belief in the imago dei in their relationships with people who tend to be despised by Christians. Maybe we'd begin to break down the impression many people have of Christ-followers as people who hate.

As a believer in creation, I'm committed to the value of all human life. I view with concern the use of abortion merely as a means of birth control. On the other hand, I view with concern the politicizing of the abortion issue, which can treat people and their deep, personal, and moral dilemmas with something less than compassion and respect.

As a believer in creation, I view with horror the tendency humans have to commit violent acts and to make war on one another—and to often minimize the loss of life by their enemies. Have we stopped to think that the lives of terrorists are as valuable to God as American lives?

As a believer in creation, I view with concern the tendency men and women have to treat members of the opposite sex without respect. In our society, women are often objects to be exploited and used—pretty things to look at, handle, and discard. But men may also be viewed as objects—as something to be manipulated by any means for a woman's own ends. When we treat our own or other people's sexuality without respect, we've lost sight of human dignity.

12. Mouw, *Uncommon Decency*, 41.

God Created Image Bearers

As a believer in creation, I'm deeply concerned about human trafficking, which is increasingly evident today. While writing this book, I learned of a couple who were arrested just north of my idealistic and high-minded city and were charged with forcing a woman from the Philippines to be a live-in worker for three years. Besides being illegal, what the couple did is wrong, especially for those who take the Bible's introduction seriously, because it violates the image of God. No person should be enslaved by another.

As a believer in creation, I can look at myself in the mirror and declare that I'm special—messed up, prone to be selfish and grouchy, and not as young as I used to be. But I'm still a creation from the hands of God. And, as someone put it, "God don't make junk!"

My brother is very interested in the economics of coffee. As a result, he's become involved with a Mexican coffee community that grows beans, roasts them, and markets them, with all the proceeds returning to that Mexican community. Each bag of Café Justo—the label for this Mexican coffee—arrives at our house sealed with the name of one of the members of that community. The product provides a sense of ownership, dignity, and respect, and it's tied to the image of God in which we're all created.

Homiletics professor Zack Eswine takes issue with preachers who start with sin, not with creation. "If we as preachers always and only start with the message of sin, without placing our sin into the context of our having been created, we discard vital aspects of the beauty of redemption." Eswine adds that "the image of God in persons reminds us that even mistaken people can do right things." He offers such biblical illustrations as the sinful woman who gives Jesus a cup of water; pluralistic philosophers who are involved in spiritual pursuit; and sinful people who show love, do good, and lend to those in need.[13] We're all creatures of dignity—a reflected dignity, yes, but one that's real.

THE IMAGE OF GOD IS REFLECTED IN OUR FREEDOM.

Why didn't God choose to create a simple universe? Why not just have rocks and algae, or creatures of instinct, such as salmon and bears? Instead, God took a risk in creating human beings. Theologian Thomas Oden writes, "The fact that God created not just inorganic matter, but human beings is clear evidence that God wished to have some part of his creation share to some degree in his own infinite freedom."[14]

God told Adam and Eve, "You may freely eat of every tree of the garden; but of the tree of the knowledge of good and evil you shall not eat" (Gen. 2:16–17). God created human beings with the capacity for choice. And with that capacity came the need for responsibility and accountability in using their freedom. If Adam and Eve chose to disobey the Creator-God's instructions, they would reap the consequences—which is what happens in Genesis 3. The playing out of those consequences is something we'll think about in the chapter "Rebellion Against Love." Nonetheless, God took the risk of imbuing us with some degree of freedom, a state that reflects God's own perfect freedom.

In Luke 15, Jesus told the parable of a loving father who gave his sons the freedom to choose whether to stay home or to leave. In that culture, sons were supposed to stay and help their father with the family farm. It would be a slap in the face for a son to leave his dear, old dad. But in the parable, one son did choose to leave the father's home

13. Eswine, *Post-Everything World*, 43.
14. Oden, *Pastoral Theology*, 228.

God Created Image Bearers

to live it up in the big city. Jesus' story radiates the sadness of the father when this son chooses to leave home, but it's a freedom the father gave to the prodigal son. This son was like many other so-called "prodigals" down through the ages who chose to thumb their noses in the father's face. Meanwhile, the other son in Jesus' story stayed home in body but not in spirit. The attitude of the older son didn't reflect the father's love and compassion. This older son was like many religious people down through the ages who chose to stay at the father's house but not to act like the father. With both sons there was a choice—freedom—and, therefore, a responsibility (Luke 15:11–32).

In Jesus' crucifixion, we confront the risk and pain God the Father accepted at the hands of rebellious human beings. The prologue to John's gospel, which rings with creation echoes, observes, "He [the Word] came to what was his own and his own people did not accept him" (John 1:11). God took a huge risk in creating us as free beings, and a huge risk in incarnating God's own self in Jesus. But how good of God to take those risks!

Today's American society is full of people who act as though everything that's wrong is someone else's fault. Many today cry out, "I'm a victim! Don't hold me responsible." But remember: We *are* created in God's image. We *are* created with at least some level of freedom. We *can* make at least some choices, and we *are* responsible for our choices.

Eastern Orthodox leader Kallistos Ware writes, "Without freedom there would be no sin. But without freedom man would not be in God's image; without freedom man would not be capable of entering into communion with God in a relationship of love."[15]

---

15. Ware, *Orthodox Way*, 59.

THE IMAGE OF GOD IS REFLECTED IN OUR STEWARDSHIP RESPONSIBILITY.

In thinking about freedom and the imago dei, we've touched on a corollary to freedom: accountability for one's actions. But there's a special kind of accountability embedded in the story of our creation—namely, stewardship responsibility.

In the first creation story, after the climax of God's creative work, the narrative describes what human beings created in God's image were to be and to do. "Let them have dominion over the fish of the sea, and over the birds of the air, and over the cattle, and over all the wild animals of the earth, and over every creeping thing that creeps upon the earth" (Gen. 1:26). That commission is repeated in God's blessing of the humans: "God blessed them and God said to them: 'Be fruitful and multiply, and fill the earth and subdue it; and have dominion'" (Gen. 1:28). Due to the commission that our Creator-God gave us as image bearers of God, we have a responsibility to be stewards of God's creation.

Having dominion, observes Victor Hamilton, commissions the human to act like a king who exercises "responsible care over that which he rules." Reflecting on the king's rule celebrated in Psalm 72:1–4, Hamilton points out that this reigning monarch is also to be "a champion of the poor and disadvantaged. . . . Even in the garden of Eden he who would be lord of all must be servant of all."[16]

God's commission for the human created in God's image is to care for the earth, where the human was placed as a representative of the Creator-God. In the second creation story we hear, "The Lord God took the man and put him in the Garden of Eden to till it and keep it" (Gen. 2:15). In Hebrew, the first of these two words of responsibility—"to till"—carries the meaning "to serve." Hamilton, echoing

---

16. Hamilton, *Book of Genesis*, 138.

God Created Image Bearers

words that Jesus applied to himself (Mark 10:45), points out, "So again the note is sounded that man is placed in the garden as servant. He is there not to be served but to serve."[17]

The image of God, then, is designed for a divine-human partnership. As image bearers, we're to represent our Creator-God in the world and join with God to tend, care for, and steward the wonderful creation that God placed in our hands. "The earth is the Lord's," sings the psalmist (Ps. 24:1). Instead of belonging to us, someone else's goods are entrusted to us. Unlike ancient pagan kings, who ravaged the earth and did with it as they pleased, we're to use creation resources in line with the purposes for which God created the resources—namely, to express and celebrate the Creator-God's character, majesty, and beauty.

In September 2011, *Time* magazine profiled "dominionists," people who "believe it their obligation to control [the hard-line term] or influence [the softer version] what are called 'the seven mountains' of business, government, media, arts and entertainment, education, family, and religion. The more extreme elements of this movement seek conquest and theocracy. Others insist they want only to transform the culture into something more in keeping with God's kingdom of justice and mercy."[18] Dominionists, particularly the hard-line version, give orthodox believers a bad name. Instead of focusing on their "seven mountains," why wouldn't they focus on the stewardship to which God's human creation was clearly called in the beginning?

Such stewardship responsibility brings accountability. Yes, we've "multiplied and filled the earth" (Gen. 1:28). But "having dominion" has all too often resulted in misusing and using up created resources. For this, we're surely accountable to our creator! In place of an image-bearing

17. Ibid., 151.
18. Meacham, "In God."

responsibility we've sometimes substituted an onerous bureaucracy of rules and regulations regarding what we can and can't do with natural resources.

THE IMAGE OF GOD IS REFLECTED IN OUR SEXUALITY.

What does the image of God have to do with sexuality? What does maleness and femaleness have to do with reflecting God? Read again this poetic verse:

> So God created humankind in his image,
> In the image of God he created them,
> Male and female he created them. (Gen. 1:27)

In Hebrew poetry, the second line, and sometimes the third line, expands on the first.

Line 1: God created Adam, the human being in God's own image.

Line 2: "In the image of God he created them." This repeats Line 1 in a slightly different form.

Line 3: "Male and female he created them." Line 3 seems to expand on line 1 and line 2.

Could these poetic lines be telling us that both males and females are image bearers and that they reflect in their maleness and femaleness something of the divine nature? That males and females in their interrelationship reflect something of the relationships within the Godhead, within the Trinity? In God, there are characteristics we tend to associate with maleness and characteristics we tend to associate with femaleness. So could it be that we need each other as men and women because we together reflect the full scope of God's image?

God Created Image Bearers

Theologian Marva Dawn comments, "Since the image of God was both male and female, we believe that in the Trinity are to be found all the best characteristics of male and female and more.... We are liberated from all stereotypes about our being male or female, for we find our own unique way of being one or the other by the way in which we image God."[19]

Typically we're oriented toward the opposite sex, as if we're magnetically charged to attract one another. True, some men and women seem oriented toward the same gender; but Genesis implies that in the beginning same-sex orientation wasn't God's creative intent.

Paul wrote to the Corinthian church, "In the Lord woman is not independent of man or man independent of woman" (1 Cor. 11:11). Does this mean that every man and every woman needs to be married? No! There's no good evidence that Jesus, the complete expression of God's image, was married. But it does mean that we need each other, men and women, to reflect the divine image completely. That's why God's design includes mothers *and* fathers. And it's surely one reason why God designed the church, the family of God, as a community of men and women bound together in covenant with God and with one another.

Remember who we're created to be. Remember the image! Let the living out of this awareness make a difference in us and in our world. In the final chapter, we'll celebrate the good news of "image renewed." Not only did God create us in God's image, but God's purpose in Christ is to renew that image, which is damaged and diseased in us.

---

19. Dawn, *In the Beginning*, 41.

APPLICATION: AS WE REFLECT ON THE IMAGE OF GOD, PRACTICE RESPECT.

Believers schooled in the Bible's introduction learn and practice respect for their fellow humans, which is based in an awareness of the image of God implanted in all of us.

Fifth-century Celtic monk Pelagius wrote, "To God nothing is so offensive, nothing so detestable as to hate anyone and to want to injure anyone; nothing is so commendable in his sight as to love everyone." Pelagius warned against what he called "the practice of disparagement," which he said "is a very grave fault, because it makes another appear worthless."[20]

Fifteen hundred years later, C. S. Lewis writes in *The Weight of Glory*:

> There are no ordinary people. You have never talked to a mere mortal. Nations, cultures, arts, civilizations—these are mortal, and their life is to ours as the life of a gnat. But it is immortals whom we joke with, work with, marry, snub, and exploit—immortal horrors or everlasting splendors. . . . Next to the Blessed Sacrament itself, your neighbor is the holiest object presented to your senses. If he is your Christian neighbor, he is holy in almost the same way, for in him also Christ . . . the glorifier and the glorified, Glory Himself, is truly hidden.[21]

Imagine the impact on our world if believers in Jesus—who take the Bible, including its introduction, seriously—actually treated all "neighbors" with respect! Imagine if we refused to identify another person merely as black or white,

---

20. Quoted in Newell, *Book of Creation*, 90.
21. Lewis, *Weight of Glory*, 9.

poor or affluent, uneducated or schooled, gay or straight, believer or nonbeliever, or even as kind or obnoxious!

While writing this book, I read *God Sleeps in Rwanda*, a sad book by Rwandan author Joseph Sebarenzi. Though Rwanda is considered one of the most Christian countries in Africa, the 1994 genocide involved the deaths of approximately one in ten Rwandans, mostly members of the Tutsi tribe. Somehow the "christianizing" of this central African country didn't include living by the understanding of imago dei that's so clearly presented in the Bible's introduction.

My wife and I also watched the movie *The Help,* based on the novel by the same name. The film effectively depicts the way whites treated African American maids in the Deep South of the 1950s and '60s. It's another sad picture to me of religious people who ignored the imago dei.

One more example: A churchgoer was irate over the fact that instead of setting up a seminar against homosexuality I decided to approach the subject of human sexuality in light of the meaning and significance of Christian marriage. "Why don't you just tell them they are an abomination to the Lord?" she raged at me over the phone. I wondered how that would help. How would that communicate the respect that's essential in our relationship with all people, whether they're gay or straight, whether their behavior troubles us or they're people we admire?

I repeat: Believers schooled in the Bible's introduction learn and practice respect for their fellow humans that's based in an awareness of the image of God implanted in all of us.

6

God Created Humans for Love

ONE MORNING IN 2004, I was eating breakfast with an eye on the *Today Show*. Host Matt Lauer was trying to make sense of a popular tabloid magazine's report that, after all the buildup and hoopla, actors Jennifer Lopez and Ben Affleck had canceled their wedding. In fact, it was reported they'd split up. She was seen at a beach in Miami; he was seen playing cards in Los Angeles. The media raised questions about who initiated the break up and whether J.Lo and Ben were ever really, really in love. Finally, Matt Lauer wondered out loud why so many people were so incredibly interested in this personal drama. I spoke back to the TV and asked Matt why *they* were taking up so much morning TV time on this sappy scenario. And nothing much has changed since then. Several years later, the media blares endless speculation about why reality-television star Kim Kardashian's marriage lasted only seventy-two-days. Did she marry for love as she said, or was it all for money?

Is this casual view of love and marriage, which is increasingly normative in our society, the way love is supposed to be? When I suggest that the Bible's introduction

God Created Humans for Love

tells us that God created human beings for love, we must change channels and reconsider what we're talking about.

But before we consider what it means that we're created for love, let's revisit the human creation story and ask a question people didn't ask in pre-scientific, ancient times.

WHO AND WHAT WERE ADAM AND EVE?

Scientists question whether the contemporary diversity of human population could've come from only one pair of humans. Bible readers also ask questions from reading the text of Genesis, such as "Who married Cain?" (Gen. 4:17); "Who were the people Cain was afraid of?" (Gen. 4:14); and "Who were these human creatures that we've come to call Adam and Eve?"

Let me suggest a way of looking at the creation of humans that begins with the second creation story (Gen. 2:4–25). Remember again that the Bible's introduction isn't a textbook on science and history, as we understand science and history. Rather, it's an ancient Middle Eastern story that contains two accounts of creation from different perspectives.

The first story in Genesis 1:26–28 tells of a sovereign God who speaks all of creation into being. Unlike that account, the second story, sometimes referred to as the Adam story, tells of God forming and shaping *adam* (earth creature) from the *adamah* (earth) and then breathing life into his nostrils (Gen. 2:7). This earth creature needs a helper/partner to fulfill God's commission to till and keep the garden (Gen. 2:15). No animal is deemed suitable as a partner (Gen. 2:20) so the earth creature (Adam)—the male-female, image-of-God-reflecting human of Genesis 1:27—is split by God into male and female creatures. Genesis 2:23 speaks of them as *ish* and *ishah* (man and woman, respectively).

75

The Story of Beginnings

Some have whimsically referred to this as God "splitting the Adam."[1] The *ish* and *ishah*, the man and the woman, are to partner together in caring for God's created garden. These *adams*, now split into fully image-of-God-reflecting male and female, are joined together in intimate oneness—the first marriage of man and woman.

Notice that the woman (*ishah*) isn't called Eve, a word resembling "living" in Hebrew (NRSV footnote), until Genesis 3:20. Adam isn't used as a personal name until Genesis 5:1 (NRSV). Could this be because, rather than being one original pair, they're representative of God's human creation?

The first story in Genesis 1 takes a different look at what God does in creating humans. In that story, the image of God is fully reflected in the male-female humanity, with an unspecified number of humans created simultaneously; the NRSV text refers to "humankind" or *adams* (earth creatures). That Genesis 1 stipulates God's creation of these *adams* as male and female doesn't require us to understand that there were only two of them. Instead, as in Genesis 2, the *ish* and *ishah* may be representative humans. At least, the story seems to open up that option to us.

WHAT ABOUT DEATH?

Were these humans created immortal, as we've often heard? God states to the *adam* regarding the forbidden tree, "In the day that you eat of it you shall die" (Gen. 2:17). But this must not mean death would immediately follow from crossing this boundary since Adam, we're told, lived to be 930 years old (Gen. 5:3). Could it be that God's human creation is potentially immortal, as suggested in God's soliloquy: "See,

1. Joy, *Bonding*, 19.

God Created Humans for Love

the man [*adam*, or "earth creature"] has become like one of us, knowing good and evil; and now, he might reach out his hand and take also from the tree of life, and eat, and live forever" (Gen. 3:22)? Could it be that they're mortal physically and that their rebellion against God results in the spiritual death of separation from God? Could it be that they weren't aware of their physical mortality until their separation from God (Gen. 3:19)?

I raise these possibilities as questions, rather than as hard-and-fast conclusions. What we can say, I suggest, is that contrary to the way we've often been told, the story doesn't require us to understand that all humans are biologically descended from one original pair who were initially created immortal. I leave a more detailed comment on the relationship between the Bible's introduction and the Apostle Paul's treatment of Adam for a later chapter. Suffice it to say at this point that—again contrary to the often-declared view—Paul's Adam doesn't require one original pair from which all have descended.

With this as background, let's return to the Creator-God's intent in forming *ish* and *ishah*—man and woman. These *adams* were to reflect the image of God, and they were created to live both in love with God and in love and community with other humans.

GOD CREATED HUMANS TO LOVE GOD.

After reading the Bible straight through, popular Christian author Philip Yancey concluded that the great book is most basically a story of God the jilted lover.[2] We hear the beginning of that love story in the Bible's introduction. But unlike the casual breakup of some self-centered movie star, in this

2. Yancey, *Disappointment With God*, 157.

The Story of Beginnings

story it's God who loves and it's the humans—the object of God's love—who have jilted the divine lover.

Try telling the story this way. Once upon a time, long, long ago, there were no people on earth. There was just God and the world of nature that God had created. There was God the Father, God the Son, and God the Holy Spirit. This Trinity was God having community within God's self. The Trinity—Father, Son, and Spirit—engaged in what theologians refer to as *perichoresis*, a Greek word that speaks of a dance. But the loving dance of the Trinity didn't seem fully to satisfy God. God wanted to share the community of the Trinity with people other than God's self. This is because the very heart of God is love. Love wants to express itself. Love wants to be in relationship, in community. So what did God do? God made a creature called a human being, who was like God, but not God, "created in the image and likeness of God." God breathed life and spirit into this created being. I wonder if God didn't say to the first human beings, "Let's be friends. Let's be partners."

In this story, the first humans, who have by now disobeyed the Creator-God's boundaries, "heard the sound of the Lord God as he was walking in the garden in the cool of the day" (Gen. 3:8). I imagine this evening walk in the garden was something God and the human pair regularly enjoyed. In hot climates, evening is the time when it cools down to tolerable. In the cool of the day, people go out for a stroll. In the cool of the morning, people go early to work. But the evening is for relationship.

Several years ago when I taught at South India Biblical Seminary for a summer, my evening ritual was first to play badminton with the men students. Then we would take a stroll down the road. I don't stroll very well. I had to work at remembering that this walk wasn't for exercise. This walk wasn't to go anywhere in particular. It was simply to be

God Created Humans for Love

together. I wonder if soon after their creation, God didn't say to Adam and Eve, "This evening how about you and I meet by that huge palm tree right next to the river?" And the evening walk became a regular thing. Why? Because that's the way God was, and that's the way God is. That's the way God created human beings—to be in a relationship of love with their creator.

When their rebellion against God makes Adam and Eve ashamed and they hide from God instead of meeting with God, God calls out, "Where are you? Where are you, my friends?" God doesn't yell at Adam and Eve, "What did you do? Why did you eat the forbidden fruit?" Instead God, the rejected lover, the one from whom the loved ones now hide, cries out "Where are you?"

We often quote Saint Augustine: "Thou hast made us [created us] for thyself and our hearts are restless till they rest in thee."[3] In the Bible's introduction, this understanding that we're created to be in relationship with God anchors who we are and how we are to live in creation. Here in this storied opening to our sacred book is the vision of a God of love creating human beings to reflect God's own self and to live in intimate relationship with God.

That's the essence of what God wants from us and for us. That's also good news that believers can share with those who don't yet believe. We're created for relationship with our loving creator. We're created to be friends, yes, even partners with God. It's a relationship in which there's no question about who is in charge, but it's still a relationship.

Unique among the religions of the world, the God of the Bible's introduction loves his human creation and wants to be loved by them. In his book *The Jesus I Never Knew*, Philip Yancey quotes Aristotle, the great philosopher of ancient Greek times: "It would be eccentric for anyone

3. Augustine, *Confessions*, 1.

The Story of Beginnings

to claim he loved Zeus [chief god of the ancient Greeks] or that Zeus loved a human being for that matter." Yancey goes on to observe about the religion of Islam, "Not once, does the Qur'an apply the word love to God."[4] On our own, human beings haven't come up with the idea of a God who loves and wants to be loved.

In sharp contrast to mere human speculation about the character of God, John's first epistle says, "Whoever does not love does not know God, because God is love" (1 John 4:8). It's not just that God loves, but that God by nature *is* love!

What does this loving Creator-God, this God of our great story, want from us? "Love the Lord your God with all your heart, and with all your soul, and with all your might," the ancient Hebrew people were told (Deut. 6:5). That, said Jesus, is the greatest commandment, along with the command to love our neighbor as ourselves (Mark 12:28–31).

Jesus said to his first followers, "I no longer call you servants, because a servant does not know his master's business. Instead, I have called you friends, for everything that I learned from my Father I have made known to you" (John 15:15). *I call you friends!* That's what God created us to be.

Frederick Buechner writes, "The power that created the universe and spun the dragonfly's wing and is beyond all other powers holds back, in love, from overpowering us."[5] Why? Because God wants our love in response to God's own great love for us. More than our service, God wants our love. In the same vein, Henri Nouwen once wrote, "The unfathomable mystery of God is that God is a Lover, who wants to be loved."[6]

---

4. Yancey, *Jesus I Never Knew*, 267.
5. Buechner, *Telling Secrets*, 28.
6. Nouwen, *Life of the Beloved*, 106.

God Created Humans for Love

God created us like himself so that we could be in relationship with God. God created us like himself so that we could share the community, even the loving dance God experiences among Father, Son, and Holy Spirit. God created human beings to love God.

GOD ALSO CREATED HUMAN BEINGS TO LIVE IN COMMUNITY WITH ONE ANOTHER.

Adam is alone, at first, in the story of the Bible's introduction. The storyteller puts these words in the mouth of the Creator-God: "It is not good for the man to be alone" (Gen. 2:18). The only thing in the creation story that God says is *not good* is Adam's aloneness. Contemporary Western people tend to romanticize this aloneness, reading into it what we understand as loneliness. But a greater key to understanding Adam's aloneness is that because of it the human can't fulfill the task of tending God's garden. As Old Testament scholar John Goldingay puts it, "Being alone means not being able to fulfill the task for which the human beings were made. He needs help. Until he has that, creation will not be 'good.'"[7]

When God goes into action again, I imagine the creator gives Adam some "anesthetic" to put him to sleep. Maybe God put Adam to sleep so that this human couldn't offer running commentary or give God advice on the creation of woman. What do you think? In the biblical story, God takes one of Adam's ribs, from which God makes a woman. When Adam wakes, there she is! Someone has suggested that nobody ever got as much out of a surgery as Adam did.

Up until now we've had no words at all reported from Adam's mouth. Maybe Adam was the original "strong,

---

7. Goldingay, *Genesis for Everyone*, 38.

silent type." But after one look at the woman God created, this previously speechless Adam breaks into poetry, the first poetry of the Bible.

> This at last is bone of my bones
> And flesh on my flesh;
> This one shall be called Woman [*ishshah*]
> For out of Man [*ish*] was this one taken.
> (Gen. 2:23)

Socrates, sage man of ancient Greek times, is reported to have said, "By all means marry. If you get a good wife, you'll become happy. If you get a bad one, you'll become a philosopher." Socrates, of course, didn't think about what would become of the woman if she got a bad husband. Socrates didn't live in the twenty-first century. Socrates also didn't live under the guidance of Genesis 1 and 2 and its high view of marriage based in mutuality and calling.

What were Adam and Eve to be to each other? The story says God created Eve because there was no suitable "helper" for Adam in his work of tending the garden (Gen. 2:18). This is the same word used in the Bible for "God is my helper." This is a high and holy kind of help, not a "go for this and that" kind of help. Eve isn't an inferior kind of person, designed only to serve Adam. As Professor Goldingay observes about Adam and Eve, "neither has authority over the other; neither is inherently the leader or the led. The image puts concretely the point made in Genesis 1, that it is men and women together who comprise the representation of God in the world."[8] Men and women in partnership together are to serve their creator and the created world. So the relationship isn't primarily romantic, but functional. The man and the woman have work to do together. They're to tend God's great garden together.

8. Ibid., 39.

God Created Humans for Love

Adam and Eve were to be helpers to each other, a holy community of mutual help. It's what God experiences in the community of the Trinity that God desires for God's human creatures. We're to live in community with one another. And by the way we live in community, we're to reflect the loving character of our God. That should be true in friendships, whether of the same gender or across gender lines. That should be true in the fellowship of the church. And that should be true in the amazing, intimate, and complex community we call marriage.

MARRIAGE IS A CALLING TO LIVE TOGETHER IN SUCH A WAY THAT GOD'S OWN CHARACTER IS REFLECTED IN OUR LIVES TOGETHER.

In marriage, according to the Genesis story, the male and female sides of God's creation join to reflect the full scope of God's image. "In the image of God created He them, male and female God created them. . . . A man will leave his father and mother and be united to his wife, and they will become one flesh" (Gen. 2:24).

This is why those who take their cue from the Bible's introduction aren't as likely to endorse same-gender marriage. We don't want to discriminate against people who desire this kind of arrangement. Rather, on the basis of the Bible's introduction, we don't accept that arrangement as marriage. If the opening story of the Bible determines how we are to view our lives and our relationships, then we confine what we call marriage to the union of a man and a woman. That was God's creative intent. Genesis 1 and 2 weigh much more heavily in my mind on this issue than the taboos and restrictions of the rest of Scripture regarding sexuality. Good people disagree on this matter, sometimes with harsh and unbecoming rhetoric. The laws of our states are changing in their understanding of marriage. I don't insist that everyone agree with my understanding on this matter. I accept that there is and will be disagreement. But while I want to be respectful, at the same time I'm called to honestly and forthrightly give witness to how I understand the Creator-God's intent for marriage.

Marriage isn't merely a concession to human sexuality, as some early church leaders thought. Marriage isn't merely a convenience so that a man and a woman can live together and have children with respectability. Marriage isn't merely a social convention or a way to deal with loneliness. Marriage, as we see it in the biblical story, is a calling—a divine calling.

Mahatma Gandhi was the man behind modern India. As with many key historical figures, Gandhi wasn't a very balanced man. Gandhi was fixated on vegetarianism, and on chastity, not only outside of but within marriage. Gandhi didn't give his marriage or his family priority in his life. Once, while Gandhi was in a South African prison, his wife, Kasturba, became very ill. Gandhi could've paid a fine, gotten out of jail, and taken care of his wife. But he declined. He tried to convince his wife that his social and political struggle against the mistreatment of Indians in South Africa was more important than her health. She pulled through and survived her serious illness. Gandhi concluded, "You cannot attach yourself to a particular woman and yet live for humanity. The two do not harmonize."

One of Gandhi's sons, Harilal, accused his celebrated father of neglecting his family, and particularly of keeping his sons ignorant by denying them education. In a letter to his father, Harilal wrote, "You have spoken to us never with love, always with anger. In argument you have always

God Created Humans for Love

used us with humiliating language."[9] Though Gandhi claimed to be influenced by the Sermon on the Mount, in this he was in direct opposition to the creation design. Unfortunately, Gandhi didn't go to the Bible's introduction when he sought to understand family relationships; he seemed to miss that humans were meant for relationships, for covenant with one another.

What might the vision of marriage offered in the Bible's introduction do for all of us who are married? What might that vision of marriage do for those who seem so ready to abandon their covenant partners because they've found someone else or want to find themselves?

Our marriages are to reflect God's character of love in community. I read once about a young farm couple in a Texas donut shop. After they were finished enjoying time together over donuts and coffee, he got up to pay the bill. But she didn't get up to follow him. The farmer came back and stood in front of his wife. She put her arms around his neck and he lifted her up, revealing that she was wearing a full-body brace. He lifted her out of her chair and backed out the front door to the pickup truck with her hanging from his neck. As he gently put her into the truck, everyone in the shop watched. No one said anything until a waitress remarked, almost reverently, "He took his vows seriously."

Marriage isn't just an arrangement I accept as long as my spouse makes me happy or until I find someone I think will make me happier. Marriage is a divine calling for a man and a woman to reflect the divine nature.

---

9. Adams, *Gandhi*, 108–12.

FOR ALL WHO FOLLOW JESUS, MARRIED OR SINGLE, TO LIVE IN COMMUNITY IS A DIVINE CALLING.

Community isn't just an option that we accept or reject. Community is a divine calling, so that in our lives together we reflect who God is. God created human beings to live in community with one another. That's why it's so important how believers treat one another. When we interact with another person, we interact with one created in the image of God like we are. When we interact with those within the faith community, our relationships should somehow reflect the character of the God who created us and who calls us into community with one another. Jesus said, "By this everyone will know that you are my disciples, if you have love for one another" (John 13:35).

Do those of us who are married fail to live up to this high and holy ideal? Do those of us who aren't married fail to live up to this ideal of life in community? Do we all fail to live up to the ideal of fully loving the God who first loved us? Do we all need to ask for forgiveness for our failures in this area? Absolutely yes! But we don't abandon the ideal just because it's high. We don't give up on the goal of wholeheartedly loving this God who first loved us because our self-centeredness so often intrudes. We don't give up on the goal of living together in community because it's so complex and demanding. These goals and ideals are part of our story. They define who we are and what we aim for.

APPLICATION: COVENANT KEEPING

The God of the Bible's introduction and of the Bible as a whole is a covenant-keeping God. To reflect this God, we as human followers of God must seriously practice covenant

God Created Humans for Love

keeping. That means we need to live in covenant relationship with God, and we need to live in explicit and implicit covenant with people in our lives.

Join me in this prayer or allow my words to trigger your own prayer.

> God, whose very nature is love, whose heart yearns for relationship,
> God, who longs to see your children bound together in community,
> We confess the ease with which we allow unloving attitudes, actions, and words to disrupt our relationships, especially with those closest to us.
> We confess the tendency to self-centeredness in our closest relationships.
> We confess the ease with which we slip toward hardness of heart.
> We pray today for all married persons.
> Give to those who are married and to those expecting to be married a God-shaped vision for marriage.
> We pray for those for whom marriage has been and is painful.
> Where there are deep wounds, bring healing and renewal of spirit.
> Before all single people, Lord, hold the image of Jesus—unmarried but complete.
> Before all who are yours—single and married—continually hold up the model of life in community with those who share the life of Christ with us.
> In the example of Jesus, may we see afresh how to give ourselves for one another.
> Hold before us once more the vision of what you desire for us as a community of oneness in Jesus.
> Amen!

7

The Blessing of Sabbath

WHAT DO WE FEEL like when we come to the end of a workweek and look back? Do we exclaim with a lot of folks, "TGIF: Thank Goodness It's Friday"? The name of a U.S.-restaurant chain capitalizes on this breathless arrival at Friday and the beginning of a weekend. I've seen posts in Facebook that say, "Friday, why did you take so long to get here?" When I was a fulltime pastor, I'd become very tired by Friday afternoon. So, I'd take Friday afternoon through Saturday off from work whenever I could. But now I wonder, when we look ahead to Sabbath—however it is that we understand Sabbath rest—how often do we celebrate not only the weekend but the week that was?

Scholar John Goldingay imagines that God, in contrast to most of us, arrives at creation's weekend "in a position to stand back, survey the six days' work as a whole, and smile in satisfaction. The project has come out very well. It looks great. If you have the chance, God's precedent suggests, plan your week's work, execute it, and then stand back and admire it."[1]

1. Goldingay, *Genesis for Everyone*, 23.

The Blessing of Sabbath

The first story in the Bible's introduction concludes with this statement: "On the seventh day God finished the work that he had done, and he rested on the seventh day from all the work that he had done. So God blessed the seventh day and hallowed it, because on it God rested from all the work that he had done in creation" (Gen. 2:2–3).

WHAT IS THE MEANING AND DERIVATION OF SABBATH?

The word *Sabbath* actually doesn't occur in the Bible's introduction. Sabbath comes from the Hebrew for "rested" or "ceased." Thus, when finished with the work of creation, God "sabbathed." Sabbath is ceasing from work and then resting, which is what the Creator-God modeled and blessed for the creation.

One commentator suggests that the blessing of Sabbath is the second climax, or highlight, of creation, with the first being the creation of the human being (Gen. 1:26–31). Note that this blessing of Sabbath is in the Bible's introduction, where, as we've observed, basic biblical themes are introduced. Thus, living on the basis of a God-blessed Sabbath—ceasing from work one day in seven—is basic to what God intends for people. Professor Goldingay observes, "Being made in God's image means working for six days like God and then stopping for one day like God. So eventually, observing the Sabbath became a distinctive marker of being an Israelite, and thus of being really committed to God."[2]

The specific word Sabbath, however, doesn't appear until "keeping Sabbath" is included in the Ten Words of Covenant, which we often call the Ten Commandments or the Decalogue. As a part of its covenant foundations,

2. Ibid., 25.

Israel is told, "Remember the Sabbath day, and keep it holy.... For in six days the Lord made heaven and earth, the sea, and all that is in them, but rested the seventh day; therefore the Lord blessed the Sabbath day and consecrated it" (Exod. 20:8, 11).

In a second version of the Decalogue given in Deuteronomy, the rationale for Sabbath is different. After a restatement of the commandment, there's this exhortation: "Remember that you were a slave in Egypt, but the Lord your God brought you out of there with a strong hand and an outstretched arm. That's why the Lord your God commands you to keep the Sabbath Day" (Deut. 5:15, CEB). Deuteronomy suggests the Sabbath is rooted not only in the creation of the world, but in the creation of the nation; both come from the hand of the Creator-God.

Ancient peoples other than the Israelites observed seven-day cycles that were connected with phases of the moon. For instance, Babylonians had their own *sabbatu*, but they were days for fasting, days of bad luck, and days on which one avoided pleasure or important projects. By contrast, Israel's seventh day wasn't associated with the cycles of celestial bodies. It was associated instead with the Creator-God, who was above the moon and stars. Thus, observes Jewish author Leon Kass, "The sanctification of the seventh day continues and completes the critique of beliefs in celestial divinities."[3]

As the great story progresses from its introduction, it becomes clear that not only is Sabbath observance one of the Ten Words of Covenant, but it's at the heart of the Hebrew people and their faith. Isaiah declares that renewed Sabbath observance will bring the people of Israel to fresh favor with God (Isa. 56:4–7). N. T. Wright comments that as Jewish people were dispersed in the ancient world, one

3. Kass, *Beginning of Wisdom*, 52.

The Blessing of Sabbath

thing their pagan neighbors knew about them was that, along with circumcision and dietary regulations, "they had a lazy day once a week."[4] Therefore, because working and waging war on the Sabbath were prohibited, enemies of Israel often chose to attack the Jewish people on that day.

Go to Israel today and you'll find a largely secular culture, but one that's still dominated by Orthodox Judaism's commitment to strict Sabbath observance. A few years ago during a visit to Jerusalem, we discovered our hotel's elevator became a "Sabbath elevator" at sundown on Friday. (A Sabbath elevator is one that automatically stops at every floor so that nobody has to work by having to operate the elevator controls.) The lobby computers also were shut down and only available at the end of Sabbath when a rabbi unlocked them. While one has to admire people taking a religious principle so seriously, is that kind of legalism what the blessing of Sabbath is really about?

N. T. Wright continues his assessment of how to respond to the blessing of Sabbath found in the Bible's introduction by referring to scholar John Walton. Walton suggests that in the ancient world, that which was built by a god was understood as a temple, or a dwelling place, for that god. What ancient people expected the god to do after six days of constructing this temple was to take up residence in it and enjoy this new home. "As with a Temple, the final part of the whole operation is when, with the structure just about complete, an image of the god himself is inserted into the shrine." In the Bible's introduction, that image is the human creation—the man and the woman created "in the image of God." "The image-bearing pair themselves is called to share in the creator's enjoyment of his world, by

---

4. Wright, *Scripture and Authority*, 144.

also keeping Sabbath. What the creator does, his image bearers will also do. They will 'take their rest' together."[5]

This creation-based vision of Sabbath redirects us from an obligation we must keep to an opportunity, a blessing, to live out what it means to be somehow like God. The picture of God blessing Sabbath, especially as told in the ancient story of Genesis, is important not just because it's to be observed, or kept, but because of what it points to: who God is and how God interacts with God's creation. Sabbath, as God's people began to recognize and codify it in their Torah, became a way of reflecting God's justice for the poor, for slaves, and even for animals. In the Sabbath year, the year of Jubilee, the poor, slaves, and animals were given opportunity to rest. Soon after the Ten Words of Covenant recorded in Exodus 20, we read, "For six days you shall do your work but on the seventh day you shall rest, so that your ox and your donkey may have relief, and your home-born slave and the resident alien may be refreshed" (Exod. 23:20–23).

Observes N. T. Wright, "The Sabbath principle is thus intimately related to the large principle of God's *justice* in the sense of God's intention—which in itself is part of a theology of creation—to put all things right at the last. . . . It is the gift of the creator to his people, particularly to the poor and the enslaved: the gift of justice itself."[6]

When the Bible's story moves into what we call the New Testament, we hear very little about Sabbath from the earliest and best-known Christian writer, the Apostle Paul. In the story of Jesus given in the gospels, our Lord seems to be regularly getting into trouble with religious leaders over his understanding of Sabbath and what was and wasn't appropriate to do on that day. It reminds me of an anecdote

5. Ibid., 140.
6. Ibid., 152.

The Blessing of Sabbath

I heard: In a Scottish highland church, where strict Sabbath observance was the norm, one of the elders pointed to how Jesus had repeatedly broken Sabbath and had spoken out against its strict observance. "Ah yes," replied another elder. "It really seems that even our blessed Lord himself was a bit of a liberal on that matter."[7]

HOW ARE WE TO BE GUIDED BY THIS THEME FOUND IN THE BIBLE'S INTRODUCTION?

Many Christ-followers agree that we aren't bound by the details of Old Testament law, including some related to Sabbath observance. But Christ-followers do affirm the guiding principles of the Bible's introduction. We believe in a creation theology, at least in theory if not in consistent implementation. How then should the storied introduction to the Bible guide our understanding and practice of Sabbath?

Some have made observing the Sabbath into an inflexible rule of life. As we've seen, Jesus ran afoul of religious leaders because he seemed to understand Sabbath as more than an inflexible rule. By contrast, many well-meaning church people have included strict Sabbath observance in a rules-based way of living. My mother used to describe how growing up in a strict pastor's family involved not even going for walks on Sunday. I remember as a youth coming to grips with the benefit a long and vigorous bike ride gave me on Sunday afternoons. Yes, it was work! But it was also a celebration of God's creation and a renewal of self for the week to come. Still, I had to work through layers of guilt before I could happily engage in a Sunday afternoon bike ride. Does that sound at all familiar?

7. Ibid., 145.

The Story of Beginnings

Here's a question: Should we observe Saturday as our "holy day," as do Seventh Day Adventists and today's Orthodox Jews? After all, Saturday *is* the seventh day of creation. If we must literally observe Sabbath, then it should be on Saturday, not Sunday. It was only after the resurrection of Jesus that Christ-followers began to meet on the first day of the week to celebrate their risen Lord (Acts 20:7; 1 Cor. 16:2).

Also, there's no evidence that early believers in Jesus transferred to their new Lord's Day the Jewish Sabbath mandate for the cessation of work. As N. T. Wright remarks, "The ordinary business of life had to go on, and we find no early Christians complaining that they were being forced to collude with pagan ways, or indeed campaigning to be allowed to keep 'their' new day in the way the Jews kept their old one."[8]

It's clear that Sabbath keeping as a legalistic obligation misses both the point of the Bible's introduction and the spirit of the new faith centered in Jesus. On the other hand, shall we largely disregard the blessing of one day in seven by rejecting what we regard as legalism? This is, in fact, our contemporary tendency (certainly more than legalistic Sabbath observance is). Does it matter whether or not we keep Sabbath at all in our modern world? Or is that really the wrong question? Isn't the Sabbath a gift and a blessing, not primarily an obligation? When religious leaders attacked Jesus for healing on the Sabbath (healing was regarded as work!), he took his criticizers back to the beginning, to the Bible's introduction. "My Father is still working, and I also am working," said Jesus (John 5:17). God's great work of caring for God's creation doesn't stop on the Sabbath, whether we keep it on Saturday or Sunday. "The Sabbath was made for humankind and not humankind for the Sabbath; so the Son of Man is lord even of the Sabbath," said Jesus (Mark 2:27).

8. Ibid., 162.

The Blessing of Sabbath

Maybe we need to step back and ask what the Bible's introduction really is saying about God working and then God blessing the time of ceasing from work, that is, resting. Legalistic obligation doesn't fit the Bible's introduction, nor does jettisoning Sabbath along with ancient dietary regulations and sundry other laws that seem peculiar to us today. How can we be guided by this introductory theme? How can we receive "the blessing of Sabbath" and accept it as a gift rather than as an obligation? To what does "the blessing of Sabbath" in the Bible's introduction point?

APPLICATION: CELEBRATE THE BLESSING OF SABBATH.

How shall we celebrate the blessing of Sabbath? I suggest three ways to think of, to celebrate, and to live in the blessing of Sabbath.

Image-of-God humans should keep a healthy rhythm of work and rest.

Work *is* good. God was creatively at work in creation. And, as Jesus said, God is still at work. But God modeled a health-giving rhythm of work and rest—that is, of ceasing from work. This way of living isn't just demanded of us, but is good for us. In *Sabbath Keeping*, author Lynne Baab quotes a self-employed woman: "I would make more money if I worked on Sunday. But I pay a personal cost for those dollars, and the tradeoff isn't worth it."[9] We live in the light of God's creative intent for us if we practice a health-giving rhythm of work and rest.

9. Baab, *Sabbath Keeping*, 33.

> Image-of-God humans allow the blessing of Sabbath to point to God as ruler of the universe and not to us.

In C. S. Lewis's novel *Perelandra,* one of the angels observes that we humans are infinitely necessary and infinitely superfluous in God's eyes. God wants us to work and serve as God's own hands and feet, partnering with God to fulfill divine purposes. At the same time, God can and will accomplish these divine purposes with or without us. God is the *ruler*, not us. Ceasing our often-frenetic activity can be a grateful acknowledgement that God, not us, is in charge.

As a local church pastor for forty-two years, I was dedicated to serving God and people. But I often struggled with the balance between what my job was and what I could gladly turn over to God. I worked consistently, if not always successfully, at keeping at least one day in seven as a Sabbath. But at times I felt guilty, even anxious about ceasing my work. After all, how could God get along without my pastoral management of people's lives and my leading the church's ministries?

When I was healthiest as a person and as a pastor was when I was able to celebrate that this was God's church, not mine. I'd give God my best. That would include working hard, but not working all the time. And then I'd gladly entrust the church and myself to God at times when I ceased from my own work. Now, as a retired pastor—whose days are structured not just by the routines of church life but primarily by my own decisions—I have to work against feeling guilty about not being forever busy. Living in the blessing of Sabbath requires working against our occasionally compulsive tendency to validate ourselves primarily through what we do. Living in the blessing of Sabbath requires us to turn over the running of not only the universe but of our small lives to our Creator-God.

The Blessing of Sabbath

So much of contemporary Western life is characterized by restlessness. We're stress-filled, anxiety-ridden, over-worked. We're worried that something will go awry if we let up on our efforts to run our lives and the world. We're too busy to accept and live in God's blessing of Sabbath. More than fifty years ago in the aftermath of World War II in Germany, scholar and preacher Helmut Thielicke delivered a series of addresses on the first chapters of the Bible titled "How the World Began," which later became a book by the same name. His words about Sabbath are relevant to us decades later:

> Above all the restlessness of our human activity, above all the striving and devising, we must keep in sight the throne of God, where he calmly and peacefully observes the Sabbath of creation. Only he who sees this throne of rest acquires the calm composure that enables him to look beyond the tumult, to the world's horizon, to the place where the enigmatical world is grounded in the higher thoughts of a heart that is thinking of us, and where the world is summoned into being by these higher thoughts."

This divine Sabbath, says Thielicke, also points to another horizon, "where on the Last Day this world will again return to Him. . . . Between these horizons of the first and the last Sabbath day of the world stands the great tranquility of God which embosoms all its unrest in his peace."[10] Again, image-of-God humans allow the blessing of Sabbath to point to God as the ruler of the universe and not to us.

---

10. Thielicke, *World Began*, 111.

> Image-of-God humans regularly come back for peace and rest in worship.

Sabbath rest, or ceasing from work, isn't just a day off. Sabbath isn't just a time to catch up on everything we've been too busy to do the rest of the week. God hallowed this time of rest and ceasing from our regular work. When God hallows something it becomes holy, devoted to God, and filled with worship.

This return to peace and rest in worship isn't just a one-day-a-week practice. A Sabbath-oriented life practices frequent "little Sabbaths." These are times when we consciously withdraw, from what Thielicke called our "restlessness," in order to refocus on God and to rest in God. Could this be what the psalmist was inviting us to when he urged, "Be still and know that I am God" (Ps. 46:10)?

Many Christ-followers today observe "the hours," regular times of relatively brief withdrawal from life's restlessness to turn to Scripture and prayer. Monks do this more extensively and in community as their pattern of life, with at least five daily worship times interwoven into their monastic work. What I personally find helpful is a regular pattern of coming before God through psalms and other Scripture, followed by a prayer walk. During the day, when internal pressures rise or when I find myself drawn toward God, I pause for a "little Sabbath." Then, the last thing I do at night, at the end of a day occupied by various kinds of work, is I cease, rest, and acknowledge God.

Lynne Baab offers a healthy and realistic correction to the tendency some of us have to be perfectionists in our observance of Sabbath. "We must let go," Baab writes, "of the sense that we can do this thing perfectly.... The Sabbath is a day to let go of my perfectionism and let God run the universe. On that day I will do my best to stop working,

The Blessing of Sabbath

let God worry about what I'm not doing right, and rest in the joy of knowing him."[11]

I close this chapter with a prayer suggested by Baab. While it's suggested for use after the Sabbath meal, it also expresses a joyful vision of God as the giver of the Sabbath gift.

> Blessed are you, Lord our God, King of the universe, who fills the entire world in his goodness—with love, kindness, and mercy. He gives food to all people, because his kindness lasts forever. May the merciful God let us inherit the Sabbath of the world to come, which will be a complete day of rest forever.[12]

---

11. Baab, *Sabbath Keeping*, 116.
12. Ibid., 127.

8

The Tempter

THE FIRST TWO CHAPTERS of the Bible close on a wonderfully high note. We see the cosmos, the garden, and the humans. God's human creations are "naked and not ashamed" (Gen. 2:25). And all of this is from the creative, good, and loving hand of God. But despite the promise of Genesis 1 and 2, it quickly becomes apparent as we move into Genesis 3—and as we look around us at contemporary life—that *all is not well with our world*.

I write this during a stint as interim pastor in the beautiful and fertile Treasure Valley of southern Idaho. One morning, I decided to walk up nearby Lizard Butte. From the top, I admired the view of the valley, including the Snake River, and the view of the mountains in the distance. From there, I walked through one of the area's many orchards and admired peaches, plums, apricots, and apples, whose growth is made possible by irrigation. As I admired these views, I thought, "Ours *is* a beautiful world!"

Some days and in some places you might think all is well with the world. But not far from my viewpoint on Lizard Butte, there's trouble. Husbands and wives fight

The Tempter

with each another and with their children. Employees get a raw deal at work. Many folks in the valley abuse drugs and alcohol, and their bodies bear the consequences of this misuse of creation. Homeless people, often treated without respect, don't know where they're going to spend the night. People steal from one another, mistreat one another out of prejudice, and break covenants of love and faithfulness. Even well-meaning churchgoers treat one another without respect and caring. All is *not* well with the world.

When I listen to the evening news, I hear of the latest casualties from Afghanistan. A million refugees from Sudan and Somalia are threatened with drought and famine. There's turmoil and bloodshed in the Middle East, with the civil war in Syria currently at the center of it. According to the United States Department of State, approximately twenty-seven million people globally are victims of human trafficking, including at least fifty thousand in the U. S. Add to this news the spate of mass shootings in America, including the terrible massacre that claimed twenty-seven lives in Newtown, Connecticut. Indeed, all is not well.

A FORESHADOWING OF DOOM.

Today, people seem more ready to recognize evil than in some previous generations. *Sin*—maybe not! After all, sin sounds rather personal. But *evil*—yes! We've reawakened to the reality of evil. Popular movies dramatize the conflict between darkness and light, evil and good. The problem is, our perception of evil is that it only seems to be found in the Mafia, or in similar bad guys. Or evil resides, depending on your viewpoint, in big banks and on Wall Street. Or in the political point of view we're opposed to—from "liberals" to "the right wing." Or, at least, in the "other guy."

The Story of Beginnings

Evil in our world has huge, cosmic manifestations. True, evil in our world is seen in the terrible crimes bad people commit. But evil is also what we sometimes see when we look inside ourselves. English author G. K. Chesterton was asked to contribute an essay on "What Is Wrong With the World?" Chesterton's offering contained only two words: "I am."[1] Are we in the image of God? Yes! But we're twisted, damaged, and diseased.

How did this all come about in the wonderful creation from the hand of God? How did this happen in a world about which God declared, "It is very good"? God's world is still good, even very good. We still sing with the psalmist, "All your works shall give thanks to you, O God," (Ps. 145:10). Still, all is not right with the world.

In the introduction to the Bible, I envision God taking the human creatures on a guided tour of the wonderful Garden of Eden. Imagine Adam and Eve reacting to the pristine beauty of the garden. "Look at the color of those flowers, that stunning waterfall, those luscious fruit!" I imagine God saying to Adam and Eve, "This is all for you. You're free to eat from any tree in the garden. *But*, you must not eat of the tree of the knowledge of good and evil. Don't eat from it. The moment you eat from that tree, you're dead" (a loose paraphrase of Genesis 2:16–17). In other words, because you're like God, you have the capacity to choose. But because you're not God, your freedom has limitations. If you don't use your God-given freedoms within boundaries God has set in place, the consequences will be very bad for you.

As we listen to the story, we see that there's going to be "trouble in River City," as the popular musical *The Music Man* puts it. There's a foreshadowing of doom. We're nervous that this wonderful story of creation is going to go south. And it does! Genesis 3 is background for the rest of human

---

1. Quoted in Van Harn, *Old Testament and Acts*, 10.

The Tempter

history. The introduction to the Bible opens the door on the reality of evil in the world. Then, in the very next chapter of Genesis, we hear the storyteller make this assessment: "Sin is lurking at the door; its desire is for you, but you must master it" (Gen. 4:9). All is not well with the world!

ENTER THE SNAKE!

I don't like snakes. The place where my parents lived during most of the time I was growing up in India was infested with cobras. One of my childhood memories is of beating a snake to death with a croquet mallet! And one of the stories my family told and retold happened before I was born. My father was coming out of the house in India, and somehow a viper fell on his shoulder. It fell to the ground without harming him, but if it had bitten him he wouldn't have survived. So it's not surprising to me that in the Bible's introduction the serpent personifies that which leads the first humans astray.

The third chapter of the story begins: "Now the serpent was more crafty than any other wild animal that the Lord God had made" (Gen. 3:1). The tendency of most readers is to leap from this sentence to a full-blown understanding of the devil, fueled by the rest of the Bible and by two thousand years of Christian thought and imagination. But here, the snake isn't given the name *Satan*, which is used elsewhere in the Bible for the adversary of God. The Bible's introduction simply talks about "the serpent."

As a pastor, I've observed that all too frequently contemporary believers see the devil under every bush and behind every problem. I've also wondered if we don't often use the devil as an excuse to weasel out of our own responsibility. "The devil made me do it!" is a very old and often-used line. Despite being made popular by comedian Flip Wilson, that line started with Eve, who told God, "The serpent tricked me..." (Gen. 3:13). While I don't think it's wise or healthy to pay too much attention to the devil, the tempter is a reality we need to deal with. I suggest we heed C. S. Lewis's classic statement: "There are two equal and opposite errors into which our race can fall about the devils. One is to disbelieve in their existence. The other is to believe and to feel an excessive and unhealthy interest in them."[2]

One good reason for not ignoring the tempter is that the introduction to the Bible doesn't do so. But how shall we understand the tempter who, in this story, takes the form of a snake? Is this tempter of Genesis 3 one and the same as the evil entity known as "the devil?" Is it the same evil one who tempts Jesus (Matt. 4:1–2), the one from whom Jesus teaches us to pray for deliverance (Matt. 6:13), the one whom Jesus saw defeated in the success of the disciples' ministry (Luke 10:18)? Is it the same evil one against whom the apostles warn us (Eph. 5:12) and who is pictured as finally defeated in the last book of the Bible (Rev. 20:1–3)? Historically, this is the most common view among Christians. For example, classic theologian Thomas Aquinas held that the devil was once the highest angel, but through pride fell and seduced humans to follow him and be his subjects.[3]

On the other hand, Jewish scholar Leon Kass understands the serpent as "one of God's creatures, [and] because he is rational, [he] acts entirely on his own, displaying that *dangerous independence* [italics added] to which he will lead the human being." The serpent, Kass observes, is "an external embodiment of certain essentially human, rational capacities."[4] These rational capacities can be used independent of the Creator-God, which Kass says is the temptation

2. Lewis, *Screwtape Letters*, 3.
3. Ferguson, Wright, and Packer, *New Dictionary*, 197.
4. Kass, *Beginning of Wisdom*, 81.

The Tempter

to which Adam and Eve were exposed. It's what led to tragedy then and leads to tragedy now.

"Now the serpent was more crafty than any other wild animal that the Lord God had made." The Genesis storyteller simply tells us it was "the serpent" that tempted Eve and Adam. As historical parable, the Bible's introduction is short on data, but it embeds ideas in its narrative that will be developed more fully in the rest of the Bible. For now, we'll leave the talking snake as undefined mystery, although I'll set the Genesis 3 snake in some of its whole-Bible context a bit later.

Suffice to say, serpents in ancient Near Eastern mythology were creatures of wisdom and of mystery. They were also often symbols of evil and of death. Now, the serpent isn't evil in itself. Genesis tells us that the snake is "one of the wild creatures the Lord God had made" (Gen. 1:21). It's not the snake that's evil. But as we'll see, the snake becomes evil's instrument to tempt humans. The important thing in the story isn't so much the snake, but the tempter whose contours are more clearly filled out in the rest of the Bible

WE HAVE AN ADVERSARY!

Genesis 3 introduces us to a tempter/adversary who's clearly neither equal with God nor coexistent with God. From elsewhere in the Bible, following Aquinas's lead, many believers see a hint that the adversary was one of God's creatures, maybe an angel, who rebelled and turned against God (Isa. 14:12). Genesis 3 doesn't give us details about the adversary. While we shouldn't push the ancient story beyond what it says, the Bible's introduction opens up the reality of temptation—that is, the temptation to rebel against the boundaries God has set for our good.

Let's fast forward from Genesis to the last book of the Bible. Revelation graphically pictures the conflict between good and evil. The conflict, says Revelation, is between God and God's forces and "the dragon, that ancient serpent, who is the devil and Satan" (Rev. 20:2). The colorful book of Revelation, full of Old Testament imagery, picks up the snake symbol of Genesis. And, says Revelation 12, this serpent-devil "is the deceiver of the whole world" (Rev. 12:9). According to Revelation 20, the business of this adversary is to deceive the nations (Rev. 20:3). Revelation uses two words to describe this evil one. He, she, or it is called the *devil*, which literally means "deceiver." This serpent-devil is also called *Satan*, literally "accuser," but also "adversary."

THE ADVERSARY'S WEAPON IS THE LIE.

This tempter's business is to deceive us, to make us believe a lie, and to live on the basis of a lie. Jesus once spoke sharply against religious leaders who wouldn't listen to truth: "You are from your father, the devil, . . . He was a murderer from the beginning and does not stand in the truth, because there is no truth in him. . . . He is a liar and the father of lies" (John 8:44).

Continue the Genesis story line to what Dietrich Bonhoeffer called "the first conversation about God."[5] I imagine the conversation about God goes something like this: "And the serpent said to the woman, 'Did God say . . . ? Did God really say, "You shall not eat from any tree in the garden?"' 'Oh no, Mr. Serpent!' says Mrs. Eve. 'We may eat of the fruit of the trees in the garden; but God said, "You shall not eat of the fruit of the tree that is in the middle of the garden, nor shall you touch it, or you shall die"'" (Gen. 3:2). The serpent

---

5. Bonhoeffer, *Creation and Fall*, 70.

The Tempter

begins the process of seducing human beings to believe and act on the basis of lies.

The story continues: "The serpent said to the woman, 'You will not die, for God knows that when you eat of it your eyes will be opened, and you will be like God, knowing good and evil'" (Gen. 3:4–5). You see, the tempter/adversary implies, God is trying to keep something really good from you. God is trying to limit you and put needless boundaries around you. God is trying to keep you from experiencing your full potential. Thus, God is really not good. So begins the lie—the untruth that is the basis of evil. The man and the woman in the Bible's introduction believed the lie and acted on it.

The voice of the tempter in the Bible's introduction foreshadows two other places in the Bible where we hear this voice. In addition to Genesis 3, in these two places the voice of the tempter is a lying voice. In the opening of the Job story, Satan, the accuser, is pictured in the presence of God. Satan asks lying questions about Job's integrity. "Does Job fear God for nothing? . . . Stretch out your hand now, and touch all that he has, and he will curse you to your face" (Job 1:9, 11). Job's behavior proves that the tempter is lying. Job refuses to curse God despite the loss of everything he has, including his health.

The second voice-of-the-tempter passage is in the familiar temptation-of-Jesus story in Luke 4:1–13. After his baptism, Jesus confronts the tempter in the wilderness. The tempter here tries to deceive Jesus into using his divine power for his own ends (by turning stones into bread), into making a deal with the tempter (by worshiping the devil as God), and into making an attention-grabbing spectacle of himself (by leaping from the temple pinnacle, knowing that angels would protect him).

The Story of Beginnings

As already noted, the Bible's introduction previews the conflict between truth and the lie, which then is described throughout the rest of the Bible. This conflict, explains the New Testament book of Ephesians, "is against the cosmic powers of this present darkness, against the spiritual forces of evil in the heavenly places" (Eph. 6:12). There's cosmic conflict between God and this tempter/adversary.

Sometimes the conflict seems very personal. It feels like the adversary is out to get *me*. The Apostle Peter described this personal conflict: "Like a roaring lion your adversary the devil prowls around, looking for someone to devour" (1 Pet. 5:8–9). C. S. Lewis provides us with a vision of the tempter as an underling devil perched on a believer's shoulder whispering lies into his ears—lies generated by the Satan, the chief adversary.[6]

When conflict with our adversary feels intense and personal, we must remember Jesus, who was the Son of God but yet was tempted by the devil. The adversary even quoted Scripture to Jesus. The devil, our deceiver, isn't above twisting truth to get us to believe a lie. When he didn't succeed in tempting Jesus to evil, Luke's tells us that the adversary "departed from him until an opportune time" (Luke 4:13). Dealing with the adversary was an ongoing struggle even for Jesus.

You and I know that dealing with the tempter is an ongoing reality of our lives. While there is within us the desire, even the longing, to live lives that are truthful, there's also within us the pull to believe and live by the lie. The lie is this: What God has said isn't true. The boundaries God has set up aren't for your good. What really matters is you. It *is* really all about you. The story of our lives, especially the story of believers' lives, is the story of deciding how to respond to this lie.

6. Lewis, *Screwtape Letters*, 1.

The Tempter

Thus, appearances notwithstanding, all is not well with the world. We do have an adversary, and our adversary's weapon is the lie.

WE CAN AND MUST DEAL WITH THE ADVERSARY.

Let me suggest three tangible ways of dealing with the adversary:

1. Pray the Lord's Prayer: "Rescue us from the Evil One" (Matt. 6:33).

That's what the Lord's Prayer literally says. We take our cue from Jesus when we move beyond thinking of evil as a force to understanding it as a more personalized "Evil One." When we pray as Jesus taught us, we're crying out for deliverance from this tempter/adversary. This isn't just a nice prayer to say together in church; it's a heartfelt cry for help! So pray along with Jesus: "Deliver us from the Evil One."

2. Follow the advice given in James 4:7: "Resist the devil and he will flee from you."

But how do we resist the devil? An old Cherokee chief once told his grandson about a battle that goes on inside people. He said, "My son, the battle is between two wolves. One wolf is Evil. It is anger, envy, greed, arrogance, self-pity, guilt, resentment, inferiority, lies, false pride, superiority, and ego. The other wolf is good. It is joy, peace, love, hope, serenity, humility, kindness, benevolence, empathy, generosity, truth, compassion, and faith." The grandson thought for a minute and then asked, "Grandfather, which wolf wins?" The old Cherokee chief simply replied, "The one you feed." We resist the devil best not merely when we desperately try

The Story of Beginnings

to say "No!" to the adversary, but when we feed the good. Pray the Lord's Prayer and resist the devil.

3. Finally, live according to truth, not according to the lie.

We deal with our lying adversary by believing and living according to truth. If the adversary is the liar, Jesus is the ultimate truth-teller. Living according to truth is living in relationship with Jesus.

However, sometimes followers of Jesus are sucked into the subtle lies of the adversary. Some of the lies about what God is like and about us include: "God only loves you when you're good." "God is really like a celestial cop, just waiting for the chance to bust you." "You're no good. You're worthless!"

My mother grew up with and lived with lies in her head. She grew up believing we could easily lose our salvation if we didn't hang on to God for dear life. My mother walked with God all her life. She was a missionary, a preacher of the Gospel, and a person who did many good works. But when she was in her eighties and very sick, she wasn't sure she was going to make it. When I visited her, she said, "Mark, I'm just not sure I can hang on to God." "Mother!" I responded in the tone that first-born sons use with their mothers. "Mother, it's not a question of your hanging on to God. The truth is God won't let go of you!" All through her life, even toward the end, the adversary accused my mother, slandered her, and tried to deceive her with lies about what God was really like.

How then does the tempter/adversary try to deceive you and me? How does this adversary work to deceive us about other people? One author describes the adversary as "dividing Christians from one another . . . subtly reinforcing stereotypes in the minds of believers who are not on guard against this, magnifying weakness and minimizing virtues to

The Tempter

produce divisive caricatures."⁷ Have we ever seen that happen? Have we seen the adversary exaggerate understandable differences among church people so that they're divided into two or more sides engaged in church warfare? That's the serpent at work! That's people believing lies about one another.

Thus, despite creation's many beauties, and despite interludes of feeling like everything is okay, all is *not* well with the world. All it takes is a tragedy, such as the massacre of children in Newtown, Connecticut, to remind us of the overwhelming reality of evil. Remember: We have a tempter, our adversary, whose primary weapon is the lie. Our life story must be one of learning to deal with our adversary's lies.

APPLICATION: THIS ADVERSARY IS A DEFEATED FOE!

The adversary was defeated in the cross and resurrection of Jesus. Though the adversary still causes trouble and still works overtime to deceive us, "the strong man," as Jesus put it, has been overpowered and bound (Matt. 12:29). The last book of the Bible makes one more thing crystal clear: We look forward to a world without evil, without an adversary. We look forward, says Revelation 21, to a city where there won't be anything unclean "nor anyone who practices abomination or falsehood" (Rev. 21:27). We live now with a great hope that encourages us to seek truth in Jesus. That great hope motivates us to live in relationship to the truth. That great hope enables us to celebrate all of God's good creation despite the adversary. According to John's first epistle, "The one who is in you is greater than the one who is in the world" (1 John 4:4). Our adversary *is* a defeated foe!

7. Lovelace, *Spiritual Life*, 138.

The Story of Beginnings

Believe it! Live daily on the basis of this reality. Don't let the tempter/adversary convince you otherwise. Surrender all your rational powers to our loving God, who sets boundaries for our good. Live on the basis of a relationship submitted to this loving God, who through the Son has, in fact, defeated the adversary.

9

Rebellion Against Love

As we've observed, something's happened since God surveyed creation and pronounced it "very good." Genesis 1 and 2 tell a wonderful story of God's initiative to create a good world and a race of image-bearing human beings. But in Genesis 4, we hear about the first murder. By Genesis 6, we hear this gloomy evaluation of the human condition: "The Lord saw that the wickedness of humankind was very great in the earth and that every inclination of the thoughts of their hearts was only evil continually" (Gen. 6:5). Centuries later, the prophet Jeremiah declared, "The heart is devious above all else; it is perverse—who can understand it?" (Jer. 17:9). Centuries beyond Jeremiah, the Apostle Paul wrote to the Romans, "Through one man sin entered the world and death through sin—and so death spread to all because all have sinned" (Rom. 5:12).

In the last chapter, we briefly surveyed the impact of the tempter in the Bible's introduction. But we also observed how counterproductive it is to play the blame game and chalk up all our woes to "the devil."

The Story of Beginnings

A few years ago, I saw a unique license plate on a car. It read simply: "Sinned." As I drove behind this person, I wondered: Is this a theological statement by a believer? I doubt it! Is this a confession? Doubt that too. Or is this a boast? Maybe.

Remember radio and television personality Art Linkletter and his conversations with children? A six-year-old told Linkletter that his favorite Bible story was the one about Jesus dying for our sins. "Why do you like that one?" Linkletter asked. "Because I sin all the time," was the child's response. "You do? How do you sin?" This precocious six-year-old regarded Linkletter sadly and confessed, "I'm a cookie stealer!"

BOUNDARIES.

One word I invite you to consider as we ponder the sad story of Genesis 3 is boundaries. To reject boundaries put in place by our Creator-God is to rebel against the relationship of loving dependence for which we're created.

Rewind for a moment to Genesis 2. Remember how God takes Adam and Eve on a tour of this wonderful Garden of Eden. Adam and Eve marvel at the flowers, the animals, the mountains and valleys, the sunrises and sunsets. I suspect Adam and Eve begin to salivate over the luscious fruit on the trees. "You are free," God told them. "You are free to eat from any tree in the garden. *But*, you must not eat of the tree of the knowledge of good and evil" (Gen. 2:16–17). Someone might ask, "Why would God do that to Adam and Eve? Why would God forbid something and make it so inviting? And what could be so wrong with the forbidden fruit?"

God's command to Adam and Eve wasn't an arbitrary prohibition. What God told them was appropriate for who

Rebellion Against Love

they were. Adam and Eve, God's human creatures, weren't God. Thus, there were boundaries around their freedoms. Fish live in water because that's the way they were created to live. Birds fly through the air because that's the way they were created. Humans were created to live in dependence on their loving Creator-God, not independently of God. God's command was a protection, a boundary, a safeguard for Adam and Eve. We were created to live in a relationship of loving dependence on our creator. Eating from the tree of the knowledge of good and evil would change all that.

Thus, these human creatures were commanded, "Don't eat of that fruit." But why not? God's response, loosely paraphrased, was: "It won't be good for you. The outcome will not be appropriate for who you are." Whenever God puts up boundaries, it isn't for God's sake, but for ours. Certain things aren't off-limits just because God arbitrarily declared them so. Certain things are off-limits because God, in wisdom and love, warns of their destructiveness to us if used outside of God's boundaries.

The great story from Genesis to Revelation tells us how the tempter tries to get us to reject these beneficial boundaries by believing and living by his lies. "Did God really say you can't eat of *any* of the fruit of the garden?" asks the serpent (Gen. 3:1). In other words, says the tempter, do you mean to tell me God has put all those luscious fruits off-limits? Why would God do that to you? Eve responds, "It's really only the tree in the center of the garden we're not supposed to touch. And we're not supposed to eat that fruit on pain of death." "Ah, but you won't really die," whispers the deceiving serpent. "In fact, you could be like God, if you ate this fruit" (Gen. 3:2–3).

Eve continues to look at the forbidden fruit, observing that it looked really, really good. Isn't it interesting that what is bad for us and outside our boundaries often looks so good? Eve begins to salivate over that forbidden fruit. She wants what's off-limits and desires whatever promises independence and self-fulfillment. So: "Eve took some fruit and ate it" (Gen. 3:6). Not only that, but she gave some of the forbidden fruit to her husband. Without questioning, Adam ate it too.

Commentator Derek Kidner writes, "Eve listened to a creature [the serpent] instead of the Creator, followed her impressions against her instructions, and made self-fulfillment her goal."[1] Hasn't the highest goal of many Americans become self-fulfillment? For instance, why do many of us get married? To be personally fulfilled. Why do many of us leave one marriage and move on to another? We think we're not fulfilled in the one marriage, so we try again in another. Why do many of us choose one job over another? The new job seems to offer greater prospects of self-fulfillment. Current book titles promise to reveal secrets of self-fulfillment. Even spirituality is often portrayed in terms of "what it'll do for me." We seek connection with God so we'll be more fulfilled—and maybe even wealthier and healthier, if we listen to some TV preachers.

Someone asks, "But what's wrong with self-fulfillment?" Self-fulfillment isn't wrong. But self-fulfillment as the chief motivator in my life uses God and uses spirituality for my own purposes. God can become just a means to my own self-centered ends. I become something other than a creature living in dependence on a loving creator. Jewish theologian Martin Buber wrote, "Something has stepped between our existence and God to shut off the light of heaven. . . . That something is in fact ourselves, our own bloated selfhood."[2]

---

1. Kidner, *Genesis*, 68.
2. Quoted in Locy and Willard, "Veneer," lines 41–42.

SELF-CENTEREDNESS.

Self-centeredness moves us to ignore boundaries that God placed in human life and motivates us to rebel against our loving Creator-God. Sin isn't just breaking rules and getting caught at it. Sin isn't just disobeying what we call the Ten Commandments (or, more accurately, the Ten Words of Covenant), which are God's guidance on how people in covenant relationship with God should live. Sin isn't just about the rules, but the relationship.

If the image of God is understood primarily in terms of relationship, the marring of that image is also understood relationally. Sin isn't just breaking a commandment; it's offending against a love relationship. Sin is opting to be independent from, instead of dependent on, the one who created us and loves us. Sin is the loved one rejecting the Lover-God.

CONSEQUENCES.

Offending against a love relationship and against a lover always involves consequences. But let's think rightly about what consequences really are. A *Far Side* cartoon depicts a very old and grey-bearded God gazing at a TV monitor. This caricatured God is watching people go by. God's finger is poised over a button with a single word on it: "Smite!" Is that view of God at all familiar?

Consequences aren't about God threatening to bust us if we don't toe the line. God doesn't say to Adam and Eve, "Eat that fruit and I will kill you." Rather, it's that there are built-in consequences to rejecting the loving wisdom of our creator. It's like a concerned parent who says, "You know, there are natural consequences to risky, harmful behaviors. If you do that, you're probably going to get hurt." It's like a physician who says, "You know, if you continue doing this or that, there will be serious consequences to your health."

Let's return to the story of Adam and Eve. The Genesis narrator tells the story very matter-of-factly. "She took of the fruit and ate. She also gave some to her husband ... and he ate" (Gen. 3:6). So here are two people enjoying a juicy piece of fruit together. Fruit juice is running down chins, arms, dripping off their elbows, like when you eat a luscious piece of watermelon. But then I think the story line slows down. Have you noticed that sometimes in a good movie, the action slows way down? Have you noticed how long the camera lingers on the characters' facial expressions? Well, as the camera pans the faces of Adam and Eve, they stop and look at each other. Suddenly, they realize that they're *stark naked*.

Not only are they naked, they're embarrassed, ashamed at not having clothes. They find ways to cover up with nearby fig leaves. The fig tree has some of the biggest leaves of any tree. Put fig leaves together and you can cover up a lot. Today, of course, the game is a little different. Today it's "see how few fig leaves you can use and still get away with it." The narrator tells us, "They hid from the Lord God among the trees of the garden" (Gen. 3:8–9). Look at them. Pretty pathetic aren't they? Dressed in roughly stitched leaf coverings, trying to hide themselves from God and each another.

But then Adam and Eve hear a sound that strikes shame into their hearts. "They heard the sound of the Lord God strolling in the garden in the evening breeze" (Gen. 3:8). Later, Genesis speaks of God strolling about with Enoch (Gen. 5:22) and with Noah (Gen. 6:9). In the beginning, it looked like God expected to be able to enjoy a relaxed walk with Adam and Eve.

"Where are you?" is the first question God asks. God doesn't call out, "What have you done," but rather, "Where

Rebellion Against Love

are you?" This isn't an angry-parent God, ready to throw the book at misbehaving children. This is rather the divine-friend God, who calls out for his created friends and is grieved that they're not where God expects to find them. As Old Testament scholar John Goldingay observes, "This is the moment when fear enters the relationship between humanity and God. There is a right kind of fear in that relationship . . . fear in the sense of reverence. . . . But we were never supposed to be afraid of the one who wants to go for a walk with us."[3]

Why do Adam and Eve hide from God? They've begun to experience the consequences of rebelling against their divine lover. Shame, fear, blaming, domineering, pain, hard labor, and death rush into the picture. Adam and Eve feel guilty for having disobeyed their divine friend.

Then the blame game begins. "You did this to me!" Adam cries out. "The woman, whom you gave me, she gave me fruit from the tree and I ate" (Gen. 3:12). So God is blamed for Adam's bad choices. Eve joins the pathetic chorus of blaming: "The serpent deceived me and I ate" (Gen. 3:13). In other words, "the devil made me do it!" And we've blamed the devil for our own bad choices ever since.

Speaking to the woman, God describes more consequences of rebellion against God. In the direct, contemporary language of *The Message*, God speaks to Eve: "You'll want to please your husband. But he'll lord it over you." When loved ones reject the Lover-God, there's also an impact on human relationships. The once-equal partnership between man and woman becomes hierarchical and domineering. "To love and to cherish" becomes "to desire and to dominate." By the time this story was told and retold among Hebrew people, patriarchy, or male-dominance, was a reality of life. But the introduction tells us that male

3. Goldingay, *Genesis for Everyone*, 49.

The Story of Beginnings

dominance wasn't what God designed. God's creative intent was for a partnership between the man and the woman, a partnership in which they helped each another fulfill God's commission to take care of the garden (Gen. 2:18). But as the Bible's introduction shows, male dominance, which still exists in much of today's world, is a consequence of the breakdown of relationship between humans and God.

Disruption in relationship with God also has an impact on our relationship with the creation. *The Message* continues: "The very ground is cursed because of you; getting food from the ground will be as painful as having babies is for your wife. . . . The ground will sprout thorns and weeds. You'll get your food the hard way . . ." (Gen. 3:16–19).

How do we feel after a demanding day at work? Often we're not just tired after a hard day's work, but so weary that the life seems sucked out of us. These are consequences of rebelling against love. Because of the way work began to be divided, "whereas a woman would especially feel the effects of human disobedience in the realm of the family and of relationships, the man would especially feel them in connection with making things grow."[4]

The Bible's third chapter closes: "The Lord God sent him [Adam] forth from the garden of Eden, to till the ground from which he was taken. He drove out the man; and at the east of the garden of Eden he placed the cherubim, and a sword flaming and turning to guard the way to the tree of life" (Gen. 3:23–24). That was the consequence of human rebellion against their loving creator. Cherubim guarding God's garden depicts the reality that we no longer live in paradise.

Today, we see consequences of human rebellion against God in the daily newspaper, on CNN, on any news Web site you check. If we're honest, we see it inside ourselves.

4. Ibid., 57.

Rebellion Against Love

We may try to deny the reality of consequences and blame someone or something else. But to be human is to experience some level of rebellion against our Creator-Lover. To be human is to experience failure to live according to this creator's loving intent. This is fundamentally what the rest of the Bible calls sin. The Bible's introduction doesn't say how every generation exhibits the same problem. It takes the Apostle Paul to make stabs at telling us how we all seem to be tainted with the same problem. But what I want to lay on the table is that we're not just talking about Adam and Eve's problem. Their story is also our story. However this condition comes about, the Apostle Paul points out, "All have sinned, and fall short of God's glory" (Rom. 3:23).

Sin is rebelling against the divine lover, failing to live within boundaries God intended.
Sin is rooted in self-centeredness, the quest for self-fulfillment above God-fulfillment. And all sin has consequences.

As noted, we often call this the Fall, though this way of describing the Genesis 3 story isn't found in the Bible's introduction. Nor do we specifically read of the Fall elsewhere in the Old and New Testaments. Rather, the term comes from a book in the Apocrypha, called 2 Esdras. Esdras, the Latin equivalent of Ezra, comments on the fact that though Adam alone sinned, his fall has implications for us all, including the lost possibility of immortality (2 Esd. 7:118).

WHAT ABOUT DEATH?

One of the theological questions regarding the Fall has to do with death. We've often understood that human beings were created immortal and became mortal upon their rebellion against God. The story tells us that death is a consequence of rebelling against God's commands. "Of the tree of the knowledge of good and evil you shall not eat, for in the day that you eat of it you shall die" (Gen. 2:17; 3:19). However, since we're told Adam lived 930 years (Gen. 5:3), this must mean some other kind of death than Adam physically dying on the spot. What kind of death is it that humans will experience as a consequence of disobeying God? *Spiritual death*, which may be another way of speaking about separation from God.

In a fascinating soliloquy, God says, "See, the man has become like one of us, knowing good and evil; and now, he might reach out his hand and take also from the tree of life, and eat, and live forever" (Gen. 3:22). The story seems to indicate that the human being is potentially immortal. But, as Paul wrote to Timothy, "It is he [God] alone who has immortality" (1 Tim. 6:16). I suggest that the storied introduction to the Bible tells us that we are mortal physically and that our rebellion against God results in spiritual death—in separation from God. Could it be that the first humans weren't aware of their physical mortality until their separation from God?

Helmut Thielicke puts it this way: "This arrogant man who wanted no limitations put upon him, this man who wanted to snatch God's eternity for himself, who wanted to be immortal and like God, *has his limitations cast into his teeth*. . . . After he has nibbled at the tree of knowledge, he will also reach out for the tree of life and plunder the fruit of immortality. . . . And therefore he is driven out of paradise and the burden of his mortality is placed on his back." So, per Thielicke, "The fact that we must depart and that our life has a terminus is therefore a reminder that we are *only* men and not God."[5]

---

5. Thielicke, *World Began*, 175.

HOW IS IT THAT ALL HUMAN BEINGS SEEM BENT TOWARD REBELLION AGAINST OUR CREATOR?

A second theological question regarding the Fall has to do with our propensity for rebellion. Saint Augustine was the first to teach that sin was somehow transmitted genetically. But Augustine's view raises red flags for contemporary people. If we understand sin primarily as a violation of relationship with God, how can we make sense of its genetic transmission? Even Paul's comparison of Adam, the original sinner, and Christ, the ultimate life-giver, doesn't require a genetic transmission of sin. Paul simply states that all who are humans (descendants of Adam) experience sin and death; that is, separation from God. But all who are one with Jesus Christ (the second Adam) through a response to grace experience life and a right relationship with God (Rom. 5:12–19). Paul speaks out of the ancient understanding of corporate humanity, which is totally foreign to our individualistic mindset. All humans were *in Adam*, our corporate ancestor. And all who respond in faith are *in Christ*, the second Adam.

Lutheran theologian George Murphy has suggested a helpful distinction between *original sin* and *sin of origin*. Peter Enns summarizes Murphy's argument: Original sin "as bequeathed to us through Augustine, refers to an event at the beginning of history and requires a historical Adam as the first human to sin and transmit that sin to all subsequent humans." Sin of origin, continues Peter Enns' summary of George Murphy, "affirms the absolute inevitability of sin that affects every human being from *their* beginnings, from birth. In other words, Murphy and others counsel that we must remain open on the ultimate origins of *why* all humans are born in sin [original sin], while resting content in the observation *that* all humans are born in sin [sin of origin]."[6] While unwilling to be dogmatic at this point, I find this at least an interim solution to this question of the Fall and its impact on us today.

THREE DETAILS CONCLUDE THE STORY (GEN. 3:20–24).

- "The man named his wife Eve . . ." (Gen. 3:20). Eve resembles the Hebrew word for living. So, says the story, "she was the mother of all who live." A unique role of women as daughters of Eve, though not an essential or necessary role, is to bear children. When I meet with young couples prior to their marriage, I raise the question of their intentions regarding children. And I observe that it's crucial that *she* be ready to have children. I remind the male partner that we men don't *have* children.

- God provides skins for clothing in place of fig leaves (Gen. 3:21). Some want to see this as prefiguring the institution of animal sacrifice. I suggest that, at its most basic level, this is an expression of mercy and care from our Creator-Lover. Animal skins work better and last longer than fig leaves do!

- Finally, God protects the tree of life by banishing humans from the Garden of Eden (Gen. 3:22–24). The Bible's introduction as story enables us to see mystery here, which we don't fully understand and can't explain. We're told in the Bible's concluding, highly symbolic book of Revelation that in the urban garden in the new creation there will be "the tree of life with its

6. Enns, *Evolution of Adam*, 124.

twelve kinds of fruit, producing its fruit each month; and the leaves of the tree are for the healing of the nations" (Rev. 22:2).

So our wonderful story has gone south. It's become a bad-news story. Loved ones have rejected and rebelled against their divine lover. What will become of the relationship between creatures and their creator? How will they deal with their failure to live according to the creator's loving intent? There's good news. Rebellion against love isn't the end of the story. There's at least a hint of good news in the Bible's introduction. I'll leave that for the next chapter.

APPLICATION: CONFESSION.

The divine friend seems to be opening the door to confession by the now shame-ridden pair. "Who told you that you were naked? Have you eaten from the tree that I commanded you not to eat from?" (Gen. 3:11). Wouldn't it have been simpler if Adam and the Eve had come clean about what they'd done? "Lord, I'm hiding because I've eaten of the forbidden fruit." But the guilty pair moves past the opportunity to confess. Thus, God pursues them: "What is this that you have done?" (Gen. 3:13).

Instead of blaming what has happened on one another or even on the adversary, we do well to practice confession of our sin. The psalmist contrasts two ways of responding to human sin, to that which most basically separates us from God. "While I kept silence [about what I'd done], my body wasted away through my groaning all day long" (Ps. 32:3). Keeping silence is like trying to hide behind fig leaves. By contrast, the psalmist declares, "Then I acknowledged my sin to you, and I did not hide my iniquity. I said, 'I will confess my transgressions to the Lord,' and you forgave the guilt of my sin" (Ps. 32:5).

Confession is not groveling or beating our breasts. Confession is most basically saying the same thing about ourselves that God says about us. Confession is acknowledging that we have been self-centered in our ignoring of boundaries, and have thus created distance between ourselves and our loving creator. The old spiritual puts it this way:

> Not my brother,
> Not my sister,
> But it's me, O Lord,
> Standin' in the need of prayer.

The First Epistle of John describes this response of confession in a Christ-centered context. After highlighting what Jesus does to cleanse us from sin, the writer continues, "If we confess our sins, he who is faithful and just will forgive us our sins and cleanse us from all unrighteousness" (1 John 1:9). It's confession that opens us to the good news hinted at in the Bible's introduction.

10

Good News of Hope

Have you gotten up early and watched the sun come up? Have you been up early enough to catch the first glimmers of dawn begin to paint the sky? The good news in the Bible's introduction is a little like the faint rays of dawn in the very early morning. The full light of day hasn't come yet. For that, we need to wait until the sun rises. Genesis 3 is full of darkness, like a night without sight of the moon. In fact, it's almost like a night without promise of the sun dawning again. But when we look and listen closely, we can catch faint rays of hope. This story isn't just about what happened, but about what God will bring to pass. And that's the basis for our hope.

However, before we celebrate this hint of hope, this glimmer of good news, let me summarize where we've been.

The Story of Beginnings

TEN THINGS I HOPE YOU'LL REMEMBER ABOUT THE BIBLE'S INTRODUCTION.

1. The Bible's introduction, in which are embedded basic themes found throughout the whole Bible, is in the genre of story, *true* story, and what one evangelical scholar calls historical parable. As an ancient story, it shouldn't be treated as a science or history textbook, as we modern people understand science and history.

2. God is the primary character of the Bible's introduction, and of the Bible as a whole. This is God, who is an eternal, personal, and relational creator.

3. The Bible's introduction doesn't tell us *how God created*, but that *God did create*. Believers may be open to the scientific likelihood that God's means of creation was a process.

4. There are other creation stories in ancient literature with similarities to the Bible's introduction. But there are also key differences, especially in the perspective on what kind of god did the creating. Remember that the story tells us light was created before the lights, that is, the sun, moon, and stars, which were worshiped in the ancient world.

5. When God completed creation, God pronounced it good, even very good. Then God engaged in Sabbath rest to celebrate God's creative work. In this, God modeled for all of us the gift of alternating work and rest.

6. God created humans uniquely to reflect the image of God, to love God, and to live in community. The imago dei—the image of God—is the most basic identity of humans to this day. As Jesus says, the commandments to love God and neighbor are the most important of all commandments (Matt. 22:34–40).

Good News of Hope

7. The first humans were commissioned to partner with God and with one another in caring for and being stewards of creation.

8. Humans heeded the tempter, who spoke through one of God's creatures, the serpent. They ignored God-given boundaries and self-centeredly rebelled against their loving creator.

9. Upon rebelling against love, humans experienced consequences of shame, guilt, separation from God, awareness of mortality, relational hierarchy in place of partnership, and problems within the creation itself. Like the first Adam, all humans experience the pull toward rebellion against love. As a result, they fail to experience God's intent for the creation.

10. As we'll explore in this final chapter, despite the rift in relationship with God, our loving creator hasn't given up on the creation. God continues to move toward *new creation* through another son of Adam, Jesus. The rest of the Bible unfolds God's new-creation purpose for humans and for the whole of creation.

A GLIMMER OF HOPE.

Pointing ahead in the Bible's great story, the Creator-God's word to the tempter opens *a ray of hope* in the tragic introductory story of the Fall.

> I will put enmity between you and the woman,
> And between your offspring and hers;
> He will strike your head,
> And you will strike his heel. (Gen. 3:15)

Old Testament commentator Derek Kidner claims that what the serpent does could be translated merely as

The Story of Beginnings

"snap at."[1] While the serpent/adversary will continue to snap at humanity's heel, the coming new Adam, Jesus, will bruise the serpent's head.

Kidner observes, "There is good New Testament authority for seeing here [in Genesis 3:15] the *protevangelium*, the first glimmer of the gospel."[2] Yes, conflict with the adversary—symbolized by the serpent striking, bruising, or merely snapping at human beings—continues and will continue. The rest of our great book is full of that story. The history of humanity is full of that conflict. But there will be a descendant of the first humans (whether or not we think they were symbolic or literal) who will strike a decisive blow against the adversary. This seed of hope is expanded in the book as a whole, growing to the full proclamation of the Good News in Jesus. The God who pointed to inklings of hope beyond the calamity that occurred in the good and beautiful world he created, that same God today points to the hope-filled story of new creation.

In his book of sermons on the Bible's introduction, theologian Helmut Thielicke writes of Jesus' ministry: "When Jesus Christ heals the sick and raises the dead the fundamental thesis behind these acts is that sickness and death should *not* exist. These things are physically unnatural . . . they are contrary to the intention, the conception of creation; they are not order but *disorder*."[3] Therefore, what we've called the Fall isn't the last word. There remains the promise of Jesus and the fulfillment of that promise in the Good News.

To believers in Colossae, the Apostle Paul wrote, "He [Jesus] disarmed the rulers and authorities and made a public example of them, triumphing over them in it" (Col.

1. Kidner, *Genesis*, 71.
2. Ibid., 70.
3. Thielicke, *World Began*, 178.

Good News of Hope

2:15). Jesus is victor over the power of evil! Paul also offered this blessing at the close of his Epistle to the Romans: "The God of peace will shortly crush Satan [or the adversary] under your feet" (Rom. 16:20).

The early church interpreted the statement in the Bible's introduction about the offspring of the woman crushing the serpent's head as a promise of Christ's victory over evil and the devil. From the late second-century, Irenaeus of Lyons writes, "Christ completely renewed all things, both taking up the battle against our enemy and crushing him who at the beginning had led us captive in Adam, trampling on his head, as you find in Genesis . . ." Irenaeus cites Galatians 3:19 as the fulfillment of this hint of promise: "But when the fullness of time was come, God sent his Son, made of a woman."[4]

Thus, embedded within the tragedy of our story is the seed of *hope*—a word to add to the previous chapter's themes of boundaries, self-centeredness, and consequences.

Note that the hint of good news isn't because Adam and Eve decide to fix things themselves. The good news isn't because Adam and Eve try hard to patch up their relationship with the Creator-God. In fact, in Genesis 4, one of Adam and Eve's offspring, Cain, brings an offering to God of the earth's produce. One way to look at this part of the story is as a human attempt to appease God and get back into the garden. Genesis 4 makes it clear that God wasn't pleased with Cain's offering. This is in contrast to an offering Cain's brother, Abel, brought from his flock. With Abel and his sacrifice, God was pleased (Gen. 4:3–5). Probably the difference isn't between an offering from the land versus an offering from the flock. The difference is most likely in the attitudes of the two givers. Cain's attitude—especially

---

4. Quoted in Louth, *Ancient Christian Commentary*, 90.

expressed in the violence he did to his brother—was unacceptable to God.

The good news isn't even that we've talked God into lightening up on the consequences of our rebellion by bringing God an offering. No, the good news is due to God's initiative, and to who God is and what God has done.

What we hear in the Bible's introduction is hope—even against the background of today's bad news. The Apostle Paul tells us that hope comes through another Adam, another human born of an earthly mother. It would be through this second Adam that Satan's head would be decisively bruised. Listen to Romans 5 in *The Message*: "You know the story of how Adam landed us in the dilemma we're in. . . . But Adam who got us into this, also points ahead to the One who will get us out of it. . . . Here it is in a nutshell: Just as one person did it wrong and got us in all this trouble with sin and death, another person did it right and got us out of it. But more than just getting us out of trouble, he got us into life."

Even in the Genesis 3 tragedy, the Bible's introduction gives us a faint preview of the Jesus story. Our Lover-Creator-God doesn't give up on rebellious humans or quit loving and seeking after his creatures. Because of what God does in Jesus, the adversary's head is crushed. Because of what God does in Jesus, there can be a restored relationship with God and new life for us all.

THE IMAGE RENEWED.

The creation stories of Genesis 1 and 2 are about the image of God created. The continuation of the second story, moving into Genesis 3, tells of the image of God marred, defaced, and damaged. We're broken people living in a broken world. In our brokenness, we don't fully live out

Good News of Hope

the Creator-God's intent for the creation. But in Genesis 3, there's at least a hint of the image of God renewed. That hint is expanded in the rest of the New Testament.

In Ephesians 4, the Apostle Paul urges believers to "clothe yourselves with the new self, created according to the likeness of God in true righteousness and holiness" (Eph. 4:24). In a parallel Colossians verse, Paul tells believers, "You have clothed yourselves with the new self, which is being renewed in knowledge according to the image of its creator" (Col. 3:10).

It's in Paul's second letter to the Corinthian church that he is clearest about what he sees God's good purpose is in new creation. "From now on, therefore, we regard no one from a human point of view. . . . So if anyone is in Christ, there is a new creation: everything old has passed away; see, everything has become new! All this is from God, who reconciled us to himself through Christ and has given us the ministry of reconciliation" (2 Cor. 5:16–18).

Today, some Christian groups seem to normalize Genesis 3 and what we call the Fall. This leaves us with hierarchy in relationships and a spoiled creation. This leaves us with nothing more than sin and its consequences to contend with. But people who take the Bible's introduction seriously insist on going back to what God intended and back to the hint of God's promise to recreate that intent.

In his book of sermons titled *How the World Began*, Helmut Thielicke states, "If I want to know who I really am and what God intended me to be, I must go back beyond the lost paradise, I must look to the morning of creation and try to hear the first words that God spoke to me and my father Adam."[5]

Rather than acting as though Genesis 3 and the story of sin with its consequences is all there is for our lives, we

5. Thielicke, *World Began*, 7.

should always look back to what the Creator-God intended and what this Redeemer-God intends for our lives today. We should look at the world, life, and ourselves through what we might call a "creation lens."

What are the implications of God's New Creation as we look out on our world and on our own lives? When believers deal with issues of sexuality, racism, war, poverty, injustice, and abortion, the big question is how we'll live out this renewed image of God. In human sexuality, for example, among followers of Jesus it's not just about whether or not we have the freedom to express our sexuality in any way that seems right to us. It really comes down to two questions: How will we live out a renewed image of God in us? And how will we value and honor the image of God in another person?

As we live in relationship with the God who created us, allowing Jesus through his Spirit to transform and recreate us daily, we're constantly being renewed in the image of God. We are and always will be people of dust. As the traditional funeral service reminds us, "From dust we were created and to dust we shall return." But we're also people with a mirror—a mirror that hopefully is being polished and cleaned so that it more and more completely reflects what we're looking at. And we have within us the glorious confidence that one day we'll be completely like Jesus—for, as John's first epistle says, "we shall see Him as He is . . ." (1 John 3:2).

For our part, the key to experiencing this hope-filled message is giving up our rebellion and accepting God's initiative toward us in Jesus. C. S. Lewis wrote, "Fallen man is not simply an imperfect creature who needs improvement: he is a rebel who must lay down his arms."[6] The key to experiencing the hope-filled good news is to cease our rebellion. Even today, the divine lover calls out, "Where are

6. Lewis, *Mere Christianity*, 56.

Good News of Hope

you? Why are you hiding?" Into our rebellion, guilt, shame, fear, blame, and domineering, our divine lover extends an invitation for us to return home. As we lay down our arms and cease our rebellion, we're reconciled to the one who has continued to love us and to seek for us. We also remain constantly open to the ongoing work of the Spirit within us: creating anew the image of God, perfectly expressed in Jesus, within our human lives.

Probably most people who read these words have had this experience of being reconciled to God through Jesus. But do we live with the hope that this reconciliation offers? Is that hope-filled message what we're sharing with our world? When people hear followers of Jesus, do they hear anger, judgment, fear, or condemnation? Or, when people hear us as followers of Jesus, do they hear hope?

In a storyteller's depiction of the Bible character Zachaeus, someone asks Zachaeus, "What did the Master say to you that night at dinner that so changed your life?" Zachaeus, this repentant tax collector, replies, "I simply looked into the deep eyes of the Master and I saw reflected there, as in a mirror, the man I could become."

APPLICATION: LET HOPE BE YOUR LIFE APPLICATION AND THE CLIMAXING WORD FROM THE BIBLE'S INTRODUCTION.

Hope is our great good news! And it begins in the Bible's introduction.

Hope is our great good news! And it's good news that our world desperately longs for and needs.

Hope is our great good news! And that hope is for us to pass on to others.

Regardless of how twisted the Bible's story has become in some of its messengers, it's most basically a good news

The Story of Beginnings

story of hope. That story begins at the very beginning, in the Bible's introduction. As we follow the story throughout the Bible, we see it's one of God never giving up on the human creation that God loves. It's a single love story, one in which the beloved is offered the hand of reconciling love by the great Lover-God. That extended hand of God is the basis for the hope we have of a new creation, not only for us as humans, but for the whole of God's creation. That new creation began in the cross and resurrection of Jesus and it continues in everyone who experiences new life in relationship with Jesus.

Once more, this time from N.T. Wright's powerful volume *Simply Christian*: "Christians are called to leave behind, in the tomb of Jesus Christ, all that belongs to the brokenness and incompleteness of the present world. It is time, in the power of the Spirit, to take up our proper role, our fully human role, as agents, heralds, and stewards of the new day that is dawning."[7]

Amen.

---

7. Wright, *Simply Christian*, 237.

Bibliography

"How was the Genesis creation story interpreted before Darwin?" No pages. Online: http://biologos.org/questions/early-interpretations-of-genesis

"What factors should be considered in determining how to approach a passage of scripture?" No pages. Online: http://biologos.org/questions/category/scripture-interpretation.

Adams, Jad. *Gandhi: The True Man Behind Modern India*. New York: Pegasus, 2011.

Augustine. *Confessions of St. Augustine*. Translated by F. J. Sheed. Indianapolis: Hackett, 2006.

Baab, Lynne M. *Sabbath Keeping*. Downers Grove, IL: InterVarsity, 2005.

Bonhoeffer, Dietrich. *Creation and Fall*. New York: Macmillan, 1937.

Brueggemann. Walter. *Theology of the Old Testament: Testimony, Dispute, Advocacy*. Minneapolis: Fortress, 1997.

Buechner, Frederick. *Telling Secrets*. New York: HarperCollins, 1991.

Collins, C. John. *Did Adam and Eve Really Exist?: Who They Were and Why Should You Care*. Wheaton, IL: Crossway, 2011.

Collins, Francis S., and Karl W. Giberson. *The Language of Science and Faith: Straight Answers to Genuine Questions*. Downers Grove, IL: InterVarsity, 2011.

Dawn, Marva. *In the Beginning, God: Creation, Culture, and the Spiritual Life*. Downers Grove, IL: InterVarsity, 2009.

Denning, Steve. "What is a story? What is narrative meaning?" No pages. Online: http://www.stevedenning.com/Business-Narrative/definitions-of-story-and-narrative.aspx.

Enns, Peter. *The Evolution of Adam*. Grand Rapids: Brazos, 2012.

Bibliography

Eswine, Zack. *Preaching to a Post-Everything World: Crafting Biblical Sermons That Connect With Our Culture*. Grand Rapids: Baker, 2008.

Ferguson, Sinclair B., David F. Wright, and J. I. Packer, eds. *New Dictionary of Theology*. Downers Grove, IL: InterVarsity, 1988.

Goldingay, John. *Genesis for Everyone: Chapters 1–16*. Louisville: Westminster John Knox, 2010.

Haarsma, Deborah B., and Loren D. Haarsma. *Origins: Christian Perspectives on Creation, Evolution, and Intelligent Design*. Grand Rapids: Faith Alive, 2011.

Hamilton, Victor P. *The Book of Genesis: Chapters 1–17*. Grand Rapids: Eerdmans, 1990.

Joy, Donald M. *Bonding: Relationships in the Image of God*. Nappanee, IN: Evangel, 1985.

Kass, Leon R. *The Beginning of Wisdom: Reading Genesis*. Chicago: University of Chicago Press, 2006.

Kelly, Gerard. *Retrofuture: Discovering Our Roots, Recharting Our Routes*. Downers Grove, IL: InterVarsity, 1999.

Kidner, Derek. *Genesis*. Downers Grove, IL: InterVarsity, 1996.

Lemcio, Eugene. "Revelation" (notes for a "Teaching of Homebuilders" class at First Free Methodist Church, Seattle, Washington, 2012).

Lewis, C. S. *Mere Christianity*. New York: HarperCollins, 1952.

———. *The Problem of Pain*. San Francisco: Harper and Row, 1996.

———. *The Screwtape Letters*. New York: HarperCollins, 1942.

———. *The Weight of Glory*. New York: HarperCollins, 1949.

Locy, Jason, and Tim Willard. "Veneer: Living Deeply in a Surface Society." No pages. Online: http://www.qideas.org/essays/veneer-a-commentary-on-culture-and-the-church.aspx?page=2.

Louth, Andrew. *Ancient Christian Commentary on Scripture*. Downers Grove, IL: InterVarsity, 2001.

Lovelace, Richard F. *Dynamics of Spiritual Life: An Evangelical Theology of Renewal*. Downers Grove, IL: InterVarsity, 1979.

McKnight, Scot. *The King Jesus Gospel*. Grand Rapids: Zondervan, 2011.

Meacham, John. "In God We Trust." *Time* (September 2011). No pages. Online: http://www.time.com/time/magazine/article/0,9171,2093314,00.html.

Middleton, Kate, and Marti Tindal, eds. *Songs for Building Community*. Kelowna, BC: Wood Lake Publishing, 2006.

Mouw, Richard J. *Uncommon Decency: Christian Civility in an Uncivil World*. Downers Grove, IL: InterVarsity, 1992.

Newell, Philip. *The Book of Creation*. New York: Paulist Press, 1999.

Bibliography

Nouwen, Henri. *Life of the Beloved: Spiritual Living in a Secular World*. New York: Crossroad, 1992.

Oden, Thomas C. *Pastoral Theology: Essentials of Ministry*. New York: HarperCollins, 1983.

Ostling, Richard N. "The Search for the Historical Adam." *Christianity Today* (June 2011) 23–25. Online: http://www.christianitytoday.com/ct/2011/june/historicaladam.html.

Peterson, Eugene. "Introduction to Genesis." *The Message*. Colorado Springs: NavPress, 2002.

———. *Answering God: The Psalms as Tools for Prayer*. San Francisco: Harper and Row, 1989.

Schaeffer, Francis A. *Escape From Reason*. London: InterVarsity, 1968.

Spina, Frank. "The Created Order." *Lectio: Guided Bible Reading*. No pages. Online: http://blog.spu.edu/lectio/genesis-11-23/.

Thielicke, Helmut. *How the World Began*. Philadelphia: Fortress, 1961.

Van Harn, Roger E., ed. *The Lectionary Commentary: The Old Testament and the Acts*. Grand Rapids: Eerdmans, 2001.

Walton, John. *The Lost World of Genesis One*. Downers Grove, IL: InterVarsity, 2009.

Ware, Kallistos. *The Orthodox Way*. Crestwood, NY: St. Vladimir's Seminary Press, 1999.

Wilkinson, David. "Bigger Than We Think." *Christianity Today* (March 2013) 27–29. Online: http://www.christianitytoday.com/ct/2013/march/bigger-than-we-think.html.

Wills, Garry. *Saint Augustine*. New York: Penguin, 1999.

Wright, N. T. *Revelation for Everyone*. Louisville: Westminster John Knox, 2011.

———. *Scripture and the Authority of God*. New York: HarperCollins, 2011.

———. *Simply Christian*. New York: HarperCollins, 2006.

Yancey, Philip. *Disappointment With God*. Grand Rapids: Zondervan, 1988.

———. *The Jesus I Never Knew*. Grand Rapids: Zondervan, 1995.

www.ingramcontent.com/pod-product-compliance
Lightning Source LLC
Chambersburg PA
CBHW071438160426
43195CB00013B/1959